# *Above and Beyond*

MERCER
UNIVERSITY

MERCER UNIVERSITY PRESS

*Endowed by*

TOM WATSON BROWN
*and*
THE WATSON-BROWN FOUNDATION, INC.

# *Above and Beyond*

## The Mason Family and the Transformation of Gwinnett County

by
Catherine M. Lewis

*Foreword by*
Sam Nunn

*Preface by*
Governor Roy E. Barnes

MERCER UNIVERSITY PRESS
*Macon, Georgia*

MUP/ H1048


Published by Mercer University Press
1501 Mercer University Drive
Macon, Georgia 31207


28 27 26 25 24    5 4 3 2 1

Books published by Mercer University Press are printed on acid-free paper that meets the requirements of the American National Standard for Information Sciences—Permanence of Paper for Printed Library Materials.

Printed and bound in CANADA.

This book is set in Bembo and Georgia.

Cover/jacket design by Burt&Burt.

ISBN 978-0-88146-945-5
Cataloging-in-Publication Data is available from the Library of Congress

# Contents

Foreword vii

Preface xii

Introduction 1

Chapter 1: The Beginnings 7

Chapter 2: An Engine for Growth 21

Chapter 3: Laying the Groundwork 40

Chapter 4: Servant Leadership 55

Chapter 5: A Rocky Road 71

Chapter 6: A New Era: From Braselton to the Beltline 83

Chapter 7: Giving Back and Passing the Torch 98

Chapter 8: Dynamic and Diverse 119

Epilogue: The World According to Wayne 131

Notes 147

Acknowledgments 171

Index 173

About the Author 183

# Foreword

*Sam Nunn*

My relationship with the Masons goes back to 1968 at the very start of my political career. I graduated from Georgia Tech and Emory University, served for six years in the US Coast Guard Reserve, and had just been elected to the Georgia General Assembly. Our family was vacationing in Daytona Beach before the session started, and I discovered that we were staying in the same hotel as Jimmy Mason. I had a chance to ask a lot of questions and get all sorts of advice about what it would be like to serve in the legislature. Jimmy was very generous with his time, and we served together for four years. He was a quiet leader, smart and thoughtful. We were both moderate Democrats from rural areas and we both cared a great deal about economic development. I was from Perry in Houston County, and he was from Snellville in Gwinnett County. Gwinnett was experiencing rapid growth.

Jimmy and I worked on a number of items together during my four years in the General House of Representatives, including on a committee charged with developing a congressional reapportionment map. We worked with Frank Pinkston in the House on a plan that we called the Mason-Pinkston plan, which passed in the House, but not the Senate, and Governor Jimmy Carter did not support it. I had just started thinking about running for Congress, and the failure of the bill to pass reshaped my political future. I didn't think I had much of a chance to win in the House of Representatives in Middle Georgia, so I turned my attention to running for the US Senate. My friend, Jimmy Mason stayed in the Georgia General Assembly for a few more years, and his brother, Wayne, became a district county commissioner in Gwinnett in 1973 and chair in 1977. They were quite the dynamic duo; they both cared deeply about looking for opportunities for growth as Gwinnett began to transition from a rural to an urban county in the metropolitan Atlanta's area.

The Masons had a lot of influence at the county and state level, and they had a good working relationship. But they could not have been more different. Jimmy was reserved, and Wayne was an extrovert with boundless energy and he was instrumental in helping propel Gwinnett into the twenty-first century. What the Mason brothers really provided was a vision for the future. They were industrious and, unlike some business and political leaders in this era, welcomed change and diversity. They had a crystal ball looking into the future and they used it.

When I think about the Masons, I'm reminded of a quote that is often attributed to Thomas Edison: "Opportunity is missed by most people because it is dressed in overalls and looks like work." Jimmy and Wayne both knew the value of hard work and what was required to get ahead and to help the community. They understood that leadership required respect for others and the ability to listen to opposing opinions. Jimmy and Wayne were not the first members of their family to embrace leadership and public service, and as their children, Keith Mason and Tracey Mason, demonstrate clearly that this ethic runs in the family.

Jimmy and Wayne also cared deeply about getting the best information to help shape their decisions. They were open-minded and curious, willing to consider all the facts before making a decision. Warren Buffet is fond of saying, "What the human being is best at doing is interpreting all new information so that their prior conclusions remain intact." The Masons' approach was the opposite, and that is because they did not fear change. They saw trends in Gwinnett, in Georgia, and in the South—about economic development, growth, and the need for new approaches and ideas—and were willing to build partnerships, invest resources, and embrace the future. Paradoxically, the Masons remind me of the story of an eighty-five-year-old man in a rocking chair sitting on his porch. A reporter came up and asked if he could interview him about what it was like to grow up in a small town. The reporter asked, "Haven't you seen a lot of change over the years?" To which the man replied, "Yep, and I've been against every one of them." That was not the Masons. Progress and improved living standards for the community and for our State was their priority. We lost Jimmy Mason far too soon, but Wayne and the rest of the family are still going strong. *Above and Beyond* tells the story of the Masons, but it's really about how a sleepy, rural county became one of the most diverse in the nation.

SAM NUNN was elected to the Georgia House of Representatives in 1968 and served as a US Senator from Georgia for twenty-four years (1972 to 1996). He chaired the Senate Armed Services Committee and the Permanent Subcommittee on Investigations. With Senator Richard Lugar (R-IN), coauthored the legislation that established the Cooperative Threat Reduction program, and the two senators were nominated for the Nobel Peace Prize in both 2000 and 2001.

# Preface

## *Governor Roy E. Barnes*

It would not be an exaggeration to say that Wayne Mason is the architect of modern Gwinnett County. In fact, the Mason family has long been in public service in Georgia, helping to shape the region for more than a century. Wayne's focus on infrastructure during his tenure as chair of the Gwinnett County Commission showed great foresight and played a significant role in the county's transformation. Gwinnett is a large county, a "mother county," if you will. Other counties were created from it, just like Fulton County was created from DeKalb. Gwinnett had a lot to offer—proximity to Atlanta, good transportation in the form of Interstate 85, and enlightened leadership that was determined to invest in the future.

When I was a child growing up in neighboring Cobb County, Gwinnett was a rural backwater. My dad farmed and ran a general merchandise business in Mableton, as did Wayne's father. As a kid, I was active in 4-H and the Future Farmers of America (FFA). I graduated from South Cobb High School in 1966, like my brother before me, and remember that the biggest thing happening in Gwinnett was the county fair, where you could show your cattle.

The Masons knew that good infrastructure was the key to smart growth. No county would thrive on septic tanks—they had to have a top-notch water and sewer system. Cities like Buford, Norcross, Lawrenceville, and Snellville were not going to attract manufacturing or industry without a reliable plan that served the whole county. The county needed wastewater treatment plants, dependable supplies of water, and good roads and bridges to attract business. The Masons saw it before anybody else, just as Ernest Barrett came to the same conclusion in Cobb County. All you had to do was look around—DeKalb boomed in the 1950s, and Cobb, Clayton, and Gwinnett were not far behind.

Jimmy and Wayne Mason predicted that Gwinnett was going to be a powerhouse county in the state and the region, and they were savvy enough to build the kind of relationships that would help it grow and thrive. They both developed close bonds with Zell Miller when he was lieutenant governor, and when he became governor, the county got plenty of attention. In the 1970s and 1980s, Gwinnett was on the cusp of explosive growth, and Jimmy and Wayne, along with other county boosters, helped usher in a new era that encouraged development in all corners of the county. These decades helped Gwinnett become one of largest and most diverse counties in the nation.

The Masons—either loved or hated—have shaped the county like no other family. Their detractors say they acted out of self-interest, but that is just not true. The Masons have public service in their blood, and they have dedicated their lives to trying to make the community they love stronger and better. The story stretches way back, and you'll get to meet a lot of characters in this book. Jimmy Mason, Wayne's older brother, was the steady hand and more of an introvert, but the two brothers made a heck of a partnership. Jimmy's life was cut short by an accident when he served on the Ports Authority, so we will never know how much more he may have contributed. To know Wayne is to love him, but you better put on your seatbelt. He has one speed—and if you want to keep up, buckle up. He talks like a machine gun and has the energy of three people. What set the Masons apart is that they dreamed big.

Jimmy and Wayne were movers and shakers, but they started with nothing. They began working as teenagers and were involved in all kinds of businesses. They made and lost fortunes in residential and commercial real estate, and they both lived a true American success story. When Gwinnett needed something, they turned to the Masons. If a new chamber of commerce building was needed, the Masons were there to help. If the county wanted a new convention center, the Masons were in the middle of it. If the city needed help with the Beltline—call Wayne Mason.

Wayne is simply a force of nature. I came to know him after I graduated from law school. He has a terrific sense of humor and a photographic memory, especially for numbers. He can calculate anything in his head in a split second. He reminds me of Bill Clinton—like a supernova. You just basked in the energy he emitted. Analyzing the growth of Gwinnett in the twentieth century through the lens of the Masons is a great way to see how people shape history. *Above and Beyond* tells the story not just of the Masons, but how a region is shaped and transformed by the people who call it home.

ROY E. BARNES is an attorney who served as the eightieth governor of Georgia from 1999 to 2003. He was a member of the Georgia Senate from 1975 to 1991 and a member of the House of Representatives from 1993 to 1999. In 2003, he was awarded the Profile in Courage Award by the John F. Kennedy Library Foundation.

# Introduction

> "I thought I was a Rockefeller for a while, but soon, I was flat broke. But I worked it off, after losing a lot of money. And I ended up paying everyone off, and then came back myself even stronger."—Wayne Mason

On March 16, 2015, Georgia senator Johnny Isakson paid tribute in the *Congressional Record* to Wayne Mason, whom he called "a great Georgian and a great friend." He went on to say, "I want to share with the Senate the greatest example I know of how much difference one man can make. I would not be where I am today and Gwinnett County—one of America's most dynamic counties—would not be what it is today were it not for the support and leadership of Wayne Mason."[1] It was a fitting seventy-fifth birthday present for a man who helped reshape an entire community.

Gwinnett County, twenty-nine miles northeast of Atlanta, has been one of the fastest growing counties in the nation since the 1980s and part of one of the largest metropolitan regions. In 2020, the census reported that the twenty-eight counties and six thousand square miles that comprise metropolitan Atlanta have a population of more than six million.[2] Nobody walking the unpaved county roads in 1900 could have imagined that Gwinnett's population would reach nearly a million residents more than a century after its founding. By 2019, the population of Gwinnett was estimated to be 936,250, making it the second-most populous county in Georgia. *Above and Beyond: The Mason Family and the Transformation of Gwinnett County* tells the story of that growth through one of its most significant families—the Masons. They first settled in Gwinnett when Redmond B. Mason took part in the 1820 land lottery, and G. F. Mason and family followed in 1838. The Masons long played a major role in the development of one of the South's largest metropolitan areas, especially after World War II. The breadth and depth of their impact truly reflects a tireless commitment to going above and beyond to help transform Gwinnett from a sleepy, agricultural county to one of the most dynamic and diverse in the nation.

The Mason family can trace its roots to the Centerville area (an unincorporated area near Snellville), which was rural and agricultural well into the 1960s, when Atlanta's population expansion powered residential development in Gwinnett. "We have deeds from the Mason-Todd house from back then," Wayne Mason explained. The family attended the nearby Zoar Methodist Church, and one of Wayne's grandfathers, Oscar Moore, served as minister of the Primitive Baptist Friendship Church on Five Forks Road for forty-seven years but "never lived long enough to see electric lights in the church."[3] The family's significance continued to grow into the twentieth century. At one point, brothers Jimmy and Wayne Mason owned 2,200 acres of contiguous land, stretching six miles from Rosebud Road east of Snellville to Georgia Highway 124 north of Snellville, with each distinct parcel connected to the next. The entire piece of land contained eleven tracts. Many of the estates that comprised their holdings were bought at auction. "On several tracts," said Wayne, "corn was growing when we bought the property. We waited for the harvest that year before we took over the land."[4] This small act of generosity illustrates a kind of empathy toward the farmers who had toiled on the land, ensuring that they would benefit from the fruits of their harvest. It also reflects how close-knit the community was in this small but growing county.

The history of Gwinnett is inextricably tied to the history of Atlanta, a city that has tripled in population and land mass in the last fifty years. As Atlanta emerged as a global transportation hub in post-World War II America, the city also became a distribution center. Its moderate climate, abundance of universities and new businesses, civil rights legacy, and appealing neighborhoods attracted newcomers. A number of major corporations (Coca-Cola, Equifax, Delta Airlines, and Home Depot) have long called Atlanta home, others (United Parcel Service and National Cash Register) moved their major national headquarters to the city. A joke often told claimed that anyone going to heaven had to make a connection through Atlanta's airport, which had become one of the busiest in the nation.

Described by Mayor William Hartsfield as "the city too busy to hate," Atlanta skirted many of the violent civil rights upheavals of the 1960s and continued to prosper while some other Southern cities, such as Little Rock, Arkansas, and Memphis, Tennessee, stagnated or shrank. As the business center continued to thrive, so, too, did the suburbs. Gwinnett County was one of the chief benefactors of that suburban growth, and the Mason family was one of the first families in real estate to capitalize on these new opportunities. The Mason brothers built their first single-family dwelling in 1959, when Dwight D. Eisenhower was president, and would go on to build 1,800 houses before shifting their focus to buying large tracts of land for commercial development. Their success reflected the county's and the region's transformation. As Gwinnett County Commission chairwoman Charlotte Nash explained, "Success bred success. Our residential and commercial boom continued unabated during the 1990s and into the 2000s. Gwinnett began to mature, becoming more urbanized and more diverse."[5]

Wayne and Jimmy Mason were instrumental in the development of Gwinnett through private investment, business development, and public service. They invested their time and talents as well as their treasure in numerous commercial and industrial development enterprises in Gwinnett and throughout the Southeast, but their biggest impact was helping build the county's infrastructure in the post-war period. Jimmy served three terms on the Snellville City Council, from 1961 to 1966. In 1966, he ran to be a state legislator and won, serving through 1974. But he was just one in a long line of Masons who held public office. Winston Mason, Jimmy's and Wayne's father, had served on the school board and helped run the school in Centerville, Georgia. Their grandfather, J. P. Mason, had been Gwinnett County's sheriff from 1938 to 1942, so community-oriented service came naturally to them. But Wayne's work on the Gwinnett County Board of Commissioners from 1972 to 1980 was transformational. During his tenure, the county secured a new water plant at Lake Lanier, paved more than eight hundred miles of roads, created a county-wide fire protection network, built Gwinnett's first modern police headquarters, and implemented its first land use plan.

The significance of these moves on the county's growth is unparalleled.

The family's commitment to public service continues through the current era. Both Keith Mason and Tracey Mason, eighth-generation residents of Gwinnett, have carried on the family's legacy. Keith, Wayne's son, while just out of high school, in 1978, coordinated Georgia lieutenant governor Zell Miller's reelection campaign in East Georgia's tenth congressional district. He then became campaign manager for Miller's successful run for governor in 1990 and served as his chief of staff until July 1993, when he left the Miller administration to work in the White House of the Clinton administration as deputy director of Intergovernmental Affairs. In that role, he was liaison between the White House and governors across the nation. In 1997, Keith returned to Atlanta to join the law firm of McKenna Long & Aldridge LLP, where he served as a public policy counselor. Today, he is CEO of KWM Capital Management LLC, a real estate and investment firm, and serves as a partner in several other private investment firms. Keith's cousin and Jimmy's oldest daughter, Tracey Mason, a product of the Gwinnett County school system, has been a longtime attorney, mediator, and Gwinnett County Superior Court judge with a deep commitment to community issues.

*Above and Beyond* is a Georgia story that reveals a great deal about the economic, business, political, and social climate in one of the South's largest and most diverse counties. Kathryn Nikolich argues in her thesis, "Gwinnett County, Georgia, A Sunbelt Community: The Invention of a Postwar Suburb," that the county was shaped by three things: "public policy, housing, and education. All three had to be in place to attract families to Gwinnett County."[6] Key members of the Mason family played an outsized role in each of those three factors. Their story is of an extraordinary family that shaped the state and the region.

# Chapter 1

## The Beginnings

> "You're not a permanent resident unless you own a cemetery lot and know where you're going to be buried."—Wayne Mason

Founded in 1818, Gwinnett County was named for Button Gwinnett, one of Georgia's three signers of the Declaration of Independence.[1] The Mason family settled in the region in the 1820s, and soon other Mason family members followed to farm, primarily cotton, like other early settlers in the county.[2] Fewer than 25 percent of the region's farmers were large plantation owners who relied on its enslaved labor force to contribute a considerable portion to the county's early wealth. That wealth would be largely destroyed by the Civil War and not rebuilt until the completion of two rail lines in the 1870s and 1880s. Gwinnett "remained a sparsely populated farming region from its founding until the late twentieth century, when Atlanta pulled the county into its orbit."[3]

There are a number of families and personalities that shaped Gwinnett over the years, and any mention of Gwinnett history will evoke the surnames Snell, Cooper, Williams, Culver, Brownlee, Nash, and Lee. More recently, longtime residents will remember stories about Charles Henry Smith, known as Bill Arp (a writer and humorist),

Buck Buchanan (a local businessman and philanthropist who would go on to lead one of Wall Street's largest brokerage firms), Scott Hudgens (a noted developer), Alice Strickland (the first female mayor in Georgia), John D. Stephens (who installed major water pipelines throughout the county), and Wayne Shackleford (who worked for Gwinnett County before being asked to lead the Georgia Department of Transportation). While all important, the Mason story provides a unique lens into the county's story over the past two centuries.

The Mason family succeeded in multiple arenas in Gwinnett throughout the county's history, including public service. Few records survive from the family's early years in the Centerville community. Various family members held public office and prominent positions in the community, but many of those stories are lost to history. Jimmy and Wayne Mason grew up in Centerville, but went to high school in Snellville, a community that was developed in 1879 when British immigrants James Sawyer and Thomas Snell started a mercantile store.[4] By the Great Depression, the generation of Wayne and Jimmy Mason's grandfathers, J. P. Mason (a former county sheriff) and Oscar Moore (a longtime minister at Friendship Primitive Baptist Church), the family had become central to the county's growth and prosperity. The family's influence would grow substantially after World War II, reshaping the very fabric of the county they had long called home. Understanding their impact requires a brief look at Gwinnett's past.

## Gwinnett's Early Years

In 1818, when James Monroe was president of the United States and William Rabun was governor of Georgia, three new counties were established and named for the three Georgians who had signed the Declaration of Independence—Button Gwinnett, Lyman Hall, and George Walton. As historian Bradley Rice explains,

> Gwinnett County lies in Georgia's upper Piedmont region astride the Eastern Continental Divide. The northwestern edge of the county along the Chattahoochee drains to the Gulf of Mexico, but the majority of the county falls in the Ocmulgee-Oconee-Altamaha basin, which drains to the main body of the Atlantic Ocean midway along the Georgia coast. The headwaters of the Yellow, Alcovy, and Apalachee Rivers rise near Lawrenceville, but they are little more than creeks until they flow further south. As a consequence, Gwinnett County lacks the sort of rich soil and well-watered bottomland that characterizes the lower Piedmont.[5]

The county is connected to the major river systems of Georgia, but most of them are mere streams in Gwinnett County. The exception is the Chattahoochee, which runs along the northern border of the county. Though the county was largely agricultural, it had poor soil and limited water resources for most of its history.

Gwinnett's founding reflected the nation's changing policy toward Native Americans in the early part of the nineteenth century. While a strategy of assimilation dominated the years leading up to and after the American Revolution, removal to the West became official policy at the turn of the nineteenth century. In the Compact of 1802, Georgia relinquished the rights to lands to the west, and the federal government promised to "extinguish the Indian title to all other lands within the State of Georgia."[6] Richard A. Cook Jr. argues in his article that "Georgia played an outside role in the story of Indian removal." Two treaties (the Cherokee Agency Treaty, signed on July 18, 1817, and the Flint River Treaty, signed on January 22, 1818) transferred Cherokee and Creek lands to the United States, setting the stage for removal. Again, Cook explains,

> Gwinnett County's land represented, at the time of its transition to American sovereignty, a frontier between tribes, between war and peace, and between assimilation and removal. By 1818 title to this land had been transferred from Native to American hands; this transfer had been negotiated through two treaties that induced Native consent by means of monetary compensation, western land exchange, debt forgiveness, and technological considerations.[7]

To the contrary, Tyler Boulware argues,

> in the 1820s and 1830s Georgia conducted a relentless campaign to remove the Cherokees. Between 1827 and 1831 the Georgia legislature extended the state's jurisdiction over Cherokee territory and set in motion a process to seize the Cherokee land, divide it into parcels, and offer the parcels in a lottery to white Georgians. The discovery of gold on Cherokee territory in 1829 further fueled the desire of Georgians to possess their land. The following year Congress passed the Indian Removal Act, which authorized U.S. president Andrew Jackson to negotiate removal treaties with Native American tribes. [John]

> Ross and other leaders fought government efforts to separate the Cherokees from their land and appealed to the U.S. Supreme Court. In *Worcester v. Georgia* (1832) the Court held that the Cherokee Indians constituted a nation holding distinct sovereign powers, but the decision would not protect the Cherokees from removal.[8]

This brutal period in American history opened the newly created Gwinnett County for white settlement, but the county's growth and development languished until the second half of the twentieth century.

Gwinnett was the fiftieth county organized in Georgia, and prior to its establishment, there was sporadic development in the area. The county covered 437 square miles and included approximately 280,000 acres of land. As Michael Gagnon details,

> In the 1820s, Gwinnett served as part of the boundary between white and Native culture. The state legislature created Gwinnett County from recently acquired Creek and Cherokee lands on December 15, 1818, adding lands from neighboring Jackson County and then requiring Gwinnett's county government to operate temporarily from Elisha Winn's property near Hog Mountain until a permanent courthouse could be built.[9]

Winn had been a justice of the peace in Jackson County, and the transfer of Jackson County lands "immediately gave the new county sufficient population to form a government."[10] Winn's home was near Dacula, and he helped make the selection for the site of the first county seat and new courthouse. For a 250-acre lot in the center of the county he paid $200. Until a permanent structure was constructed in 1824, county business was held in a log cabin. In 1821, when Gwinnett still consisted of just a cluster of agrarian communities, Lawrenceville (named for the War of 1812 naval hero Captain James Lawrence) was incorporated and designated the county seat. Primarily agricultural, Gwinnett's main industry was cotton, and farming, with or without the use of enslaved labor, built the community's early wealth.[11]

Growth in the county was somewhat restricted by the means of travel in that era prior to railroads. In the 1840s, a stagecoach line ran from the depot at Stone Mountain, due east of Atlanta's downtown by about ten miles, to Gainesville by way of Lawrenceville, a distance of approximately seventy miles. The trip took ten hours to complete and ran three days a week, with return trips the other three days. Gwinnett differed from its sister metropolitan Atlanta counties in some significant ways: DeKalb, Cobb, and Clayton Counties had rail lines as early as the 1840s, thus linking them to the young, fast-growing city of Atlanta. But as Bradley Rice explains,

> railroads did not reach Gwinnett until 1871, six years after the Civil War. Even then, the first line in the county bypassed the tiny county seat village of Lawrenceville. Unlike many of Georgia's counties, Gwinnett lacked a central identity revolving around a dominant county seat town where almost all the economic and political elite resided and interacted. Several small towns in Gwinnett, especially those along the county's two late nineteenth-century railroad lines, served their immediate trading areas, but not much more.[12]

## Slavery, Secession, and the Civil War

Like many rural communities in the South, Gwinnett relied, to some degree, on slave labor before the Civil War. Gwinnett County was unique because it was both "western and southern at its origins."[13] Historian Michael Gagnon explains that Gwinnett was in the "transition zone from cotton plantations to the Upcountry. South and east of Gwinnett lies the Plantation Belt, where enslaved African Americans usually equaled or outnumbered the white population."[14] Gwinnett was an amalgam of "plantations, yeoman farmers, sharecroppers, and renters, as well as poor whites without land who served as farm laborers."[15] The first mention of slavery in the county is found in the 1820 census, which documented that 23 percent of households included enslaved persons. Gagnon explains, "Those households averaged a median of two slaves each, and the enslaved people accounted for nearly 12 percent of the county's total population." That number grew to 25 percent of households by 1830, largely because of a gold rush.[16] By 1860, on the eve of the Civil War, 76 percent of the county's farms were producing cotton, and, 21 percent of households owned a median of four slaves.[17] The 1860 census showed a population of 12,940, with 2,441 enslaved men and women. Many small farmers could not afford a larger number of slaves, but those who did profited from the use of enslaved labor.[18] In comparison to other counties, such as Walton and Newton, Gwinnett's enslaved population never became a majority. It would be more like DeKalb, Hall, and Jackson Counties in that respect.[19]

Gwinnett County's experience of the Civil War was also unique, as historian Keith Hebert argues: "Most Gwinnett County residents opposed secession and the Confederate government that it produced. Prior to the January 2, 1861, statewide election for delegates for an upcoming secession convention, Gwinnett County leaders had gained notoriety for their opposition to secession."[20] Their opposition had nothing to do with wanting to end slavery; rather, they "viewed slavery as a national institution best protected under the U.S. Constitution."[21] Their perspective was shared by Alexander Hamilton Stephens, an influential Georgia politician who would serve as vice president of the Confederate States of America (CSA) during the Civil War. Gwinnett would eventually send three delegates, James P. Simmons, Richard D. Winn (son of Elisha Winn), and Thomas P. Hudson, to the state capital to vote on whether to remain in the Union. All three men voted against secession, but the secessionists won the vote 208–89. In the aftermath, Simmons offered the following resolution:

> We, the undersigned delegates to the convention of the State of Georgia now in session...most solemnly protest against the action of the majority in adopting an ordinance for the immediate and separate secession of this state, and would have preferred a policy of cooperation with our Southern sister states. Yet, as good citizens, we yield to the will of the majority of her people, as expressed by their representatives; and we hereby pledge our lives, our fortunes, and our sacred honor to the defense of Georgia, if necessary, against hostile invasion from any source whatever.[22]

After secession, more than 1,100 local men volunteered to serve in the Confederacy, and "Gwinnett County raised twelve companies of infantry, five companies of cavalry, and one artillery battery. Enlistment rates in Gwinnett mirrored patterns found elsewhere across the Confederacy."[23] But there were also a number of residents who were Unionists, resisted enlistment, or deserted. While not the site of any Civil War battles, the county found that both invading Union soldiers and Confederates were disruptive to their livelihoods. Confederate scouts and impressment agents were more than willing to steal from county residents, and the situation became more acute in the last year of the war. Historian Keith Hebert explains, "During the summer of 1864, three large American armies encircled Atlanta. Both armies looked to Gwinnett County for valuable supplies, especially fodder for their horses."[24] As Kirby explains, "Wiley Webb, a landowner and farmer near the Rosebud community, for example, was one of the heavy losers, according to published accounts. He not only lost his stock, cattle, hogs, and sheep, but also 300 bales of cotton, which the Yankees burned."[25] Historian J. C. Flanigan writes in his first volume of *History of Gwinnett County*, "Bands of men past the age for service in the army, and boys too young, were organized to protect the county from Sherman's army. These were called scouts, or home guards, or rangers, while Sherman's foragers were called bummers. There were numerous skirmishes in the western part of the county between these two groups of soldiers." Flanigan recounts an incident in which US troops

> passed along Rockbridge Road by Trickum and, as they approached a dwelling, later the homeplace of

> James W. Andrews, the crack of a rifle gave notice that danger lurked nearby. Another shot brought the second enemy to the ground. In all, five Yankees were killed. A man by the name of Goldsmith had concealed himself in a log smokehouse, and it was he who shot the foragers. The enemy soon located the smokehouse, set fire to it, and Goldsmith met a horrible death.[26]

Most county residents welcomed the Confederacy's surrender in April 1865, but they would continue to grapple with the damage wrought by the Civil War and seek to rebuild their lives and fortunes. Newly freed enslaved men and women sought assistance from the Freedman's Bureau but continued to experience violence and racism during Reconstruction, evidenced by a riot at Gobey's School (near Sugar Hill), in July 1868, when a group of drunken whites attacked the students and parents celebrating.[27] The lynchings of Peter Coffee, William Coffee, Isham Harbin, Thomas Martin, Charlie Hale, and Mart McConnell were reminders to African Americans of the precarious and dangerous position in which they found themselves in the South after the Civil War.

## The Magic of the Railroads

Rebuilding from the war would take decades, and, as historian R. Scott Huffard Jr. explains,

> like much of the South, the Civil War constituted a decisive turning point for Gwinnett County's economic history. Gwinnett's boosters connected their arguments to a broader narrative of regional revival—the New South movement. As the New South story

> went, the South was ready to cast aside remnants of its economic past—mainly plantation slavery—and embrace a new industrial economy that would take advantage of the South's ample natural resources. New South boosters promoted textile mills, lumbering, coal mines, and steel production, but without ample rail transportation, those dreams would never come to fruition.

Much of the wealth in Gwinnett before the war was destroyed and would not be rebuilt until the completion of two rail lines (the Southern Railroad in 1871 and Seaboard Air Line Railroad in 1892). Huffard notes, "Gwinnett County's lust for the magic of new railroads echoed the experience of the South at large in the decades after the Civil War. As railroad construction surged and mileage doubled over the course of the 1880s, boosters like Henry Grady heralded the dawn of a New South."[28] These new rail lines helped lead to the development of towns like Dacula and Lilburn, and "beyond these two main lines, entrepreneurs constructed a narrow gauge track—a branch line off of the southern corridor between Suwanee and Lawrenceville—that was completed in 1881."[29] The Loganville-Lawrenceville (L&L) Railroad was founded in 1898, and the ten-mile rail connected the Seaboard and a spur went off in Lawrenceville went south to Grayson and then on to Loganville.

For Gwinnett, railroads in the nineteenth century were transformational in the same ways that highways and suburbanization would become in the twentieth century. New lines meant the expansion of existing towns and the formation of new ones. The Richmond Air Line spawned the cities of Norcross, Suwanee, Duluth, and Buford while the

Seaboard Air Line helped expand Carl, Auburn, Dacula, Gloster, Luxomni, Lilburn, and Grayson.[30] Lawrenceville, the county seat, suffered when it lost its textile mill during the Civil War but continued to grow in this period. The courthouse was burned in 1871 by the Ku Klux Klan as they sought to destroy evidence of their failure to pay taxes on moonshine. The new courthouse was deemed inadequate after only twelve years and was replaced in 1885 at a cost of $23,000 by the building now known as the Historic Courthouse. That building continued to serve as the county courthouse until 1988 when a new courthouse was constructed. The Gwinnett Historic Courthouse, listed on the National Register of Historic Places in 1980, remains the centerpiece of downtown Lawrenceville and today houses the Gwinnett Historical Society and the Gwinnett Veterans Memorial Museum.[31]

The county's first major industry came in 1868 when the R. H. Allen Tannery was established, possibly at the Elisha Winn house that Robert Allen appears to have been renting before setting up in Buford. Robert's brother, Bona, soon followed with the Bona Allen Tannery, which later purchased the R. H. Allen Company after Robert's death. Both tanneries made leather goods such as harnesses, whips, and shoes and became famous for handmade saddles. Other businesses soon followed, including those funded by Buck Buchanan, who helped "transform Norcross from a popular summertime resort to a regional manufacturing center." He brought the Buchanan Plow and Implement Company, United Electrical Manufacturing, and Nor-X car company to Norcross. He would also help found the city's library, waterworks, and electric system, and helped finance a boulevard linking Norcross with Peachtree Road.[32]

Like so many counties, Gwinnett is an amalgam of towns and cities that had multiple names, appeared on maps before they were chartered or incorporated, or evolved from smaller communities. They include Lawrenceville (1821); Norcross (1870); Buford (1872); Duluth, first called Howell's Crossroads (1876); Grayson, first called Trip (1881); Loganville (1887); Dacula, originally called Hoke (1905); Lilburn, first called McDaniel (1910); Braselton (1916); Snellville (1923); Rest Haven (1938); Sugar Hill (1939); Suwanee (1949); Berkeley Lake (1956); and Auburn (1982).[33] Sugar Hill has the best story about how it got its name. According to the city's website,

> many years ago, Buford was a railhead from which several freight wagons traveled regularly to Cumming, which even today has no rail lines. The story is that on one of the freight trips, a heavily loaded wagon lost a wheel on a high hill and spilled a part of its load, including several large bags of sugar. The wheel was repaired, and the wagon reloaded—except for the sugar, which had broken open and spilled on the hill. The area became know as "the hill where the sugar spilled." It was shortened to "The Sugar Hill" and then just to "Sugar Hill." Sugar Hill existed as a Georgia Military District for many years before it was chartered as a city on March 24, 1939.[34]

On the eve of the twentieth century, Gwinnett remained largely agricultural with a small population that, in 1900, had reached 25,585 people, while the city of Atlanta had grown to 89,872 residents.[35] It would take two more generations and significant changes to the county's infrastructure, managed in part by Wayne Mason, to position Gwinnett for the kind of growth that the county would experience in the last fifty years.

# Chapter 2

# An Engine for Growth

> "You appreciate what you've got if you made it yourself." —Wayne Mason

Atlanta's growth in the early twentieth century was explosive, but Gwinnett, not thirty miles north of downtown, was on a different trajectory. This sleepy county "was open land, a few stores offering nothing more tantalizing than an occasional tin of canned salmon or sardines imported from the west, and small-time farmers and their wives who clung to the red clay with unmatched tenacity."[1] While the South was booming in this era, Gwinnett was still mostly rural and peripheral to the New South ethos that shaped Atlanta.

*Atlanta Constitution* editor Henry Grady (1850–1889) is credited with promoting the concept of "The New South" in the pages of the paper. As Darren Grem argues,

> Grady preached the promises of a New South, arguing that slavery and secession were dead in the region, and that northern financial help would aid reconciliation between former enemies while turning a profit. He also urged northerners to allow white southerners to manage the rights of Black citizens. Though these ideas were not original to Grady, his advocacy of unity and trust between the North and South helped to spur northern investment in Atlanta industries.[2]

His ideas were not universally applauded, and farmers and populists like Tom Watson (1856–1922) were critical of Grady's willingness to promote reconciliation and industrial and economic development. But Grady's boosterism and willingness to serve as the New South's primary spokesman prevailed and would shape the region for the next half century.[3]

By 1900, Gwinnett's population was 25,585, spurred on by the completion of the railroads in the county.[4] The county's first major industry was leather, and Buford became a hub. The Bona Allen Harness and Saddle Factory, founded in 1873 on Main Street, became one of the major producers of hand-tooled saddles and bridles. At one point, it employed 2,400 workers. Gene Autry and the cast of *Bonanza* had saddles made there. Singer and actor Roy Rogers (1911–1998) visited the growing city often to be fitted for new saddles. The city of Buford honored Rogers and saddle maker John Johnson in 2006 with a statue of the two men and Rogers's horse, Trigger, in a downtown park.[5] The factory remained in operation until the 1930s, and the building burned in December of 1981. Part of the tannery became the Tannery Row Artist Colony, which is where Buford artist Vic McCallum sculpted the statue of Rogers.[6]

Reflecting on the county's changes,

> in 1906, Gwinnett representatives to the legislature sought to control operation of the newfangled automobiles beginning to appear on the county roads. Among the guidelines they enacted: it was unlawful to go over 10 miles per hour; a motorist approaching anyone riding or driving a horse or mule was required to stop within 100 yards and shut off his ma-

> chinery until the horse or mule passed; when coming upon a horse or mule from behind, an automobile driver was required to blow his horn or whistle, then allow the four-legged animal to be unhitched or give it time to get out of the way.[7]

Still largely agricultural, Gwinnett felt the threat of the boll weevil—insects in the beetle family that can destroy cotton crops—and dropping cotton prices, which prompted a shift from cotton to dairy farming throughout the region in the early twentieth century. As William D. Bryan states, "A USDA study found that while 93 percent of a select group of Gwinnett farmers were able to make a profit growing cotton prior to 1895, by the 1920s only a quarter of all farmers came out ahead due to sharp drops in cotton prices."[8] Efforts by the government and scientific groups to encourage farmers to move away from cotton dominated the 1920s and 1930s and encouraged diversification throughout Gwinnett. Some turned to other crops or dairy production, some migrated to the North and Midwest, and others sold their land to developers, which helped begin the process of suburbanization.

## Growing Up Gwinnett

The Mason family had been in Gwinnett County since Andrew Jackson was president. Ellery James Mason, Wayne Mason's great-grandfather, had been a respected farmer in the county. Mary Almanza Lee, his wife, was the sister of James Wideman Lee, a well-known Methodist minister and bishop who later became head of the Methodist Conference. He led Trinity Methodist Church and was an advocate for interfaith dialogue. Lee, who was close friends with

"Uncle Remus" creator Joel Chandler Harris and newspaper editor Henry Grady, helped integrate the YMCA, gave a eulogy on the centennial of Abraham Lincoln's birthday, and spoke at Grady's funeral.[9] He was also the father of Ivy Ledbetter Lee (1877–1934), who is credited as a pioneer in the field of modern public relations. A graduate of Princeton, Ivy Lee worked as a reporter in New York and made a name for himself as a spokesperson for the Pennsylvania Railroad Company and later for John D. Rockefeller. His willingness to talk openly to the press was innovative, and Jared Meade, writing for *PR News*, explains that Lee "helped shape the public's perception of the profession. He also set standards that practitioners continue to follow to this day." This included his 1906 "Declaration of Principles," which was the "first document to embed ethics into the practice of PR."[10]

Wayne's and Jimmy's maternal grandfather, Oscar Moore, was a respected Primitive Baptist minister at Friendship Church (on Dogwood Road and Five Forks Trickum Road) and Camp Creek Baptist Church in Lilburn. He died in 1947, and as Wayne Mason remembered, "He never saw electric lights. They always had lanterns in the house. He also believed that President Franklin D. Roosevelt walked on water."[11] Their paternal grandfather, J. P. Mason, was a farmer who sold his crops at curb markets on Auburn Avenue and Dekalb Avenue along with his wife, Emma, who made pies and cakes. J. P. was also a businessman, the justice of the peace in the South Rockbidge district, and sheriff of Gwinnett County from 1938 to 1942. Wayne recalled that

> he was one of the most influential men in town and worked hard to help people save their farms during

> the Great Depression. Every time a farm faced foreclosure, J. P. bought notes and let his neighbors keep the land. He saved a big part of the county. He also served as a justice of the peace and lived to be 86 years old. His sister, Addie was a Deshong, who had 1,700 acres in Gwinnett and DeKalb counties right below Stone Mountain. Her husband accumulated the land during the Great Depression but failed to keep up with the taxes. J. P. went to the courthouse to pay the back taxes and returned the land to his sister. I remember that he always used cash, he was never willing to take on any kind of debt. That was a powerful early lesson for me. I loved watching how he operated, and it taught me a lot. If you got land you can always get money.[12]

Jimmy and Wayne Mason grew up in Gwinnett County when it was still sparsely populated and primarily agricultural. Jimmy was born in Centerville on January 26, 1937, and Wayne on March 22, 1940, just as the nation was trying to pull itself out of the Depression. Jimmy had a twin, Oscar Farrell, who did not survive the birth. They also had an older sister, Winifred, who worked as a homemaker and had three children, two daughters and a son. She married Alan Herndon, a University of Georgia graduate who was commissioned in the army and stationed in Germany. When they returned home, Alan worked first as a teacher. He then took a job at National Service Industries and worked at ZEP Enterprises for Erwin Zaban, who was often called "the godfather" of the Jewish community in Atlanta.

Gaye, the younger sister, married Gary Ewing. Gaye played a critical role in the Masons becoming involved in politics outside of their immediate community. She attended Young Harris College and was a student of Zell Miller's, who was a professor of history and political science. Miller served as the mayor of Young Harris from 1959 to 1960 and completed two years in the Georgia Senate (1961–1964). When he ran for Congress in 1964, Gaye and her fellow students Hank Huckaby and Marti Pingrey Fullerton worked on his campaign.[13] As Keith Mason recalled,

> That was the beginning of Zell Miller's relationship to our family. Miller ran against Phil Landrum, and he was not popular in Gwinnett because he signed a labor bill, the Landrum-Griffin Act, and the union members put their support behind Miller. My uncle, Jimmy, worked at Southern Bell, and Miller campaigned hard in Gwinnett. One day he saw Jimmy working on a telephone pole. He stopped and waited for him to come down and asked for his support. My uncle was impressed and told him he'd have the support of the whole Mason family. He did, and I would go on to work for Miller in high school.[14]

Miller eventually lost the 1964 election, but he would go on to serve as chief of staff for Georgia governor Lester Maddox (1967–1971), Georgia Democratic Party director under Governor Carter (1971–1973), four-term lieutenant governor (1975–1991), two-term governor (1991–1999), and US Senator (2000–2004).

Jimmy graduated from Snellville High School in 1954, and Wayne from South Gwinnett High in 1958. Wayne had a lifelong struggle with dyslexia and was held back in the first grade. Frustrated that he was behind his peers, he later used the money he earned to hire tutors in the summers to catch up, thus graduating high school in three years.

Wayne had $1,750 in the bank on graduation day, and his senior yearbook has a photograph captioned "I don't like money, but it does quiet my nerves."[15] After graduation, Wayne went to work for his uncle, S. Courtland Williams, painting houses on Clairmont and Lavista roads in Atlanta, where he learned how to manage construction projects. He recalled, "When I started building, I knew I could hire all those guys—the brick masons, painters, carpenters, floor layers. It was a fast crew."[16]

Jimmy's and Wayne's parents were James Winston "Wink" Mason and Ida Belle Moore Mason, who was one of ten children. Before World War II, the family moved to Avondale Estates, and Wink worked as a streetcar conductor. During the war, he took a job at Bell Aircraft, which later became Lockheed, in Marietta, and moved his wife and children back to the family farm while he drove fellow war workers to the plant every day. Wayne recalled, "My father would leave at four A.M., work all day as a machinist, and not come back until after dark. He always drove a load of people to and from the plant."[17] Wink held a number of jobs—schoolteacher, farmer, streetcar driver in Kirkwood, and worker at General Shoe Factory in Lawrenceville. The latter position was too dangerous, so he decided to go work for General Motors in their parts and service division in Doraville, overseeing their inventory. He remained at GM until his retirement in the 1970s. He also coached basketball and baseball. Ida Belle was a schoolteacher in Sugar Hill, in the northern part of the county, and at Rockbridge Elementary in the small community of Centerville. Wayne remembered, "She had nine surviving siblings and was a gregarious and charming woman who had terrific people skills. I also remember that she loved to cook pies."[18]

Much of Wayne's success was rooted in his childhood. When he was twelve years old, his father gave him ten dollars. That would be the last money he would take from his parents. From that point forward, he and his brother earned their own way through sheer determination and hard work. Describing one of his many enterprises, Wayne explained,

> I would plow gardens around Centerville, behind a one-eyed mule. I was so small that I had a sled to haul my plows. Before I went out, I had my three different types of plows fixed on the sled, since I was not big enough to rig them myself. I had one plow for the middle or rows of gardens, one for beans and another for corn. I was not tall enough to reach the plow handles to pick it up, nor strong enough to bend down and turn the plow around on the ground, then drag it to the next row. That old one-eyed mule would watch me and wait until I got the plow ready and knew when to take off. Families had small gardens, with the men working in town most of the day, so they paid me to plow their gardens. I charged all of them the same thing, a dollar, no matter what the size of the garden. It might be half an acre or an acre.[19]

Plowing was only one of his ventures. Recalling how he parlayed his farm life into a steady stream of income and eventually his life's work, Wayne said,

> I did everything. I was raised on a farm, and we'd grow stuff. We'd save vines and wrap them with cedar for wreaths and sell them at Christmas. And then, I sold stuff all over Atlanta. I sold eggs, delivering

> them all over town. Those rich people, they'd feel sorry for me and in the winter I'd go into their house—my little hands would be cold and red, and they'd give me a pair of gloves. Some Saturdays, I might get 10 pairs. Then I'd go to school on Monday morning and sell them to the other kids. What did I need gloves for? You can't count eggs wearing gloves. I sold people anything they wanted to buy, whether it was pine straw, horse manure out of the barn, or red clay. Whatever they wanted, I sold [them]. And I painted houses and made a dollar-and-a-quarter an hour. In the summer, I worked construction and that's how I learned to build houses.[20]

Wayne, like all of the Masons before him, prized self-sufficiency and proudly bought all of his own clothes and paid for his lunch at school. He explained, "On Mondays, I always made sure that I had a $10 bill to use to pay for my lunches that week. Meals in those days cost at first 75 cents a week, then went eventually to $1.25 a week. Many a time the teachers had to run all around school to make change for my $10 bill. I made people think I had money, whether I had made $10 in the last week or not."[21] Wayne always remembered that Jimmy was a better student and even skipped a grade, but Wayne was voted "Most Likely to Succeed" in high school. In 1955, Wayne lied about his age to get a driver's license and started working for Hubert Brannen, who distributed auto parts.[22] He recalled,

> I worked all over North Georgia when I was about 17, spending three days a week delivering auto parts. Brannen didn't sell tires, so I could buy tires and sell them to the same places where I was delivering auto parts. Goodyear gave me the lowest price they had

> on tires, and I got a free re-cap every time I sold 10 tires. So I sold the tires at what I paid for them, and then sold that re-cap for $10. Every time I sold 100 tires for Goodyear; the re-caps made me $100. Soon I was buying so many tires from Goodyear that they wanted me to go work for them. I did, and soon I was their top salesman. I sold more tires than anybody for Goodyear in the Southern Region in 1959.[23]

That same year he married his wife, Ann. They had met years earlier in high school on a blind date; as she remembered,

> a very close friend of mine in high school was dating a boy from near where Wayne lived. His older sister and my older sister were good friends and in the same class, and I knew Jimmy. But somehow, I never met Wayne. I did see him one day playing basketball, and my friend told me we should go out on a date. I didn't want to because he walked across the court like he owned it, and I thought he was stuck up. But he talked me into it, and we had a blind date at Stone Mountain. We dated on and off for five years, and eventually got married in 1959. We first lived in Avondale Estates in a large apartment that we rented for eighty dollars a month, then moved to Snellville. We built the house we live in now in 1965 and moved in that next year.[24]

Jimmy and Wayne could not have been more different. As Wayne's son, Keith Mason, recalled,

> Jimmy was known for his crew cut, and that never changed. He had thick hair, multiple cowlicks, and kept it short to keep it under control. He fought and

> was injured in Korea (1957–1959) and started working for Southern Bell when he returned home. He was the first one of the brothers to run for public office. If you had to characterize them, you might say that Dad was the business guy, Jimmy was the political and community guy. They were like yin and yang, but made a great team.[25]

Richard Tucker, who started working with the Masons in 1972, remembers something similar: "They were night and day. Jimmy was the gregarious politician of the two. Wayne was all business and had great instincts. I always felt that people want you to do well, but not too well. They will forgive you anything but making money. That was Wayne—he had a knack for making money and was not without his detractors. But they were as close as brothers can be."[26] Martha Byrd, who worked as the Mason brothers' assistant for thirty years, used to say, "If one of them had 15 cents, he'd give 7 ½ cents to the other. And if the other one needed the whole 15 cents, he'd give him the whole thing."[27]

## Growth and Lawlessness

During the Masons' formative years, Gwinnett County and the entire metropolitan Atlanta region went through a dramatic transformation. Bill Kirby writes, in his book *Dynamic Gwinnett*, "After the Great Depression and World War II, paved roads and jobs lured people into Atlanta to work. But they came home at night, and, to the casual observer, Gwinnett was no different. Atlanta was only an office or a factory. Lawrenceville, Snellville, Buford, and Lilburn were home. Folks were urban by day and rural by night."[28] Early medical facilities were built in the county, and the first small hospital opened in Duluth on July 9, 1944. As Elliott Brack explains, "More than 500 people were at its dedication that summer. The hospital was far larger, now consisting of 20 rooms, plus administrative, examination, emergency, and operating facilities."[29] Other clinics sprang up throughout the county, and a county-funded facility did not come to Gwinnett until 1959.[30] Tracey Mason recalls,

> Dr. Miles Mason Jr. (grandson of Elery James Mason, cousin of Jimmy and Wayne) was instrumental in the early operations of the Duluth Hospital. His son, Dr. Miles Mason III, later became a Chief of Staff at Gwinnett Medical Center. The Mason Clinic was a partnership between the County Health Department and local hospitals that began providing primary care for indigent children under the age of 16 in 1996. Its name honors Dr. Miles Mason Jr., known as "Daddy Mason" who was associated with helping the uninsured in Gwinnett.... They both are direct descendants of Elery James Mason, cousins to Jimmy and Wayne.[31]

The Masons grew up near Snellville, a town in Gwinnett that was chartered in 1923, just a few years after the end of World War I. But the town's roots go further back: Englishmen Thomas Snell and James Sawyer founded Snellville in the 1870s and set up a mercantile business together at what would become US Highway 78 and State Route 124. Several churches also date from that earlier time. The 1920 census put Gwinnett's population at 30,327 and Snellville's at about 600. Emmett Clower, who grew up in Snellville, remembered the main intersection in town at that time: "We've got a painting here that shows the intersection, made in 1952, and, in fact, [Highway] 124 was dirt. If you were going to Lawrenceville, it stopped up there at Alexander Park and then you went on the old North Road into Lawrenceville." He remembered that city hall and the fire station were one building that also doubled as the jail and council meeting rooms.[32] The Masons played a significant role in the development of the town as the City of Snellville's website explains, "In the late 1950s two local brothers, Jimmy and Wayne Mason, began building homes in the Snellville area. With the availability of attractive, affordable brick homes, Snellville grew more than 200 percent. Shopping centers, hospitals, schools and churches appeared to meet the needs of the growing population. The Masons were very active in recruiting doctors, dentists, grocery chains, etc. to stimulate the growth."[33] Barbara Bender, who later became mayor, recalled that Highway 124 "was all horse farms and a two-lane road for a long time. Then it got widened and the properties sold off.... That's when everything kind of left 78 and went up to 124." The town that was once so small that the mayor doubled as the traffic court judge was poised to grow in ways that its founders never could have imagined. Towns like Snellville throughout Gwinnett would have continued to grow, but not at the rate they did without a major catalyst.

After World War II, the construction of Buford Dam and Lake Lanier had a profound effect on Gwinnett County. The US Army Corps of Engineers had been studying the Apalachicola-Chattahoochee-Flint River systems since before World War I, but the plan to build a dam in Buford did not materialize until after World War II.[34] By the early

1940s, Atlanta mayor William Hartsfield was constantly promoting the city, as journalist Henry Grady had done before him, and he "implored Georgia's congressional delegation to support the river development plan" because it would be vital for the growth of Atlanta.[35] Hartsfield understood better than anyone that water would be the key to the development of the state's fastest growing city, and that its impact would drive growth, transportation, and industry throughout the metropolitan region. During World War II, "federal defense funds poured into metropolitan Atlanta," and Fort McPherson (East Point) and Bell Aircraft Corporation (Marietta) expanded just as military installations did in Columbus, Augusta, and Savannah.[36] Hartsfield looked "upon the dam as the first step, built to regulate water, that could eventually lead to other dams and a river connecting Atlanta by barge to the Gulf of Mexico."[37] The Rivers and Harbors Act of 1946 started the process of building the dam, which depended on congressional appropriations. As historian Deanna Gillespie explains, "Hartsfield, [Rep. James C.] Davis, and other supporters skillfully shepherded the project through a labyrinth of congressional subcommittees to secure needed appropriations."[38] In 1947, Congress allocated $250,000 for planning and another $750,000 two years later to extend planning and begin construction.[39]

As Gillespie writes,

> On March 1, 1950, a crowd gathered on a hill overlooking the Chattahoochee River in northern Gwinnett County. It was not easy to reach the relatively remote spot after overnight rain turned the dirt roads to mud. Despite this, approximately five thousand people crowded around the grandstand. At

> 11:00 A.M., the band from nearby North Georgia College played the national anthem. As the music ended, Atlanta mayor William B. Hartsfield, Georgia governor Herman E. Talmadge, and other visiting dignitaries took center stage. One by one, they took turns describing the historical significance of the day's festivities. The ceremony marked the groundbreaking for a massive federally-funded public works project that would, in Hartsfield's words, "revolutionize life in the Chattahoochee basin."[40]

Hartsfield was right; no public works project shaped the region quite like the Buford Dam and Lake Lanier. Both "powered Atlanta's postwar emergence as an unofficial Sunbelt capital, serving as a vital hub for transportation and commerce."[41] The dam ushered "northeastern Georgia into the modern age" and solidified the sense that "the dam and northeastern Georgia's future [were] intertwined with Atlanta's."[42] Construction of the dam between Gwinnett and Forsyth Counties began in 1954 at a cost a total of $45 million. More than half went to design and construction (56 percent), with the remaining budget set aside for the purchase of land and relocation costs.[43]

After years of planning, Buford Dam was completed in 1956, and the intake gates were closed. As Elliott Brack explains, "It took three years for the waters to reach the normal pool level of 1,070 feet."[44] Lake Lanier, named for Georgia poet Sidney Lanier, was dedicated on October 9, 1957. Representative John S. Wood was quoted in the *Gainesville Times* saying, "The Buford Dam...one of the largest in the Nation, will mean an immediate economic gain to the people of our area, and its future benefits to our section of the state promise to be large."[45]

Managing water in the county would be a major enterprise. Katheryn Nikolich argues,

> The infrastructure that Gwinnett County needed to control was lowland flooding and upland erosion that occurred from the Yellow River. In 1954, the County Commissioners, Paul Dover, O. D. Cain, and Weldon B. Archer, applied for federal resources to the Watershed Protection and Flood Prevention that was included in Public Law 566.... Under this law, Gwinnett County received funds to build fourteen dams between the years 1965 to 1980. In 1965, the first three dams were built at Brush Fork Creek, Numbers 3, 22, and 25. Two years later a fourth dam at Brushy Fork Creek, Number 21, was built followed by two more in the Upper Mulberry River, Number 11 in 1976 and Number 7 four years later.[46]

Wayne Mason came of age during this period, building his first house in 1959 with his older brother, Jimmy, and he always said that water was the key to his success.

But this growth was overshadowed by the county's reputation for lawlessness. There were plenty of unsavory aspects of the county's history, including an incident at the Buford Rock Quarry Prison for Incorrigibles. In 1956, in protest of their treatment and brutal working conditions, more than thirty prisoners broke their own legs with sledgehammers, prompting an investigation and coverage in the national media. The August 13 issue of *Time* magazine reported that "beyond dispute was the fact that the inmates of Rock Quarry had sunk so low on the scale of human hope that they had ducked out of the searing sun into the shadow of a rock pile, had smashed each other's legs in a despairing gesture of mass protest" because they had been "driven to their madness by the brutality of prison bosses."[47] One inmate recalled,

> I was sitting there on the ledge watching them. They laid their legs across two stones. Three men came down the line with hammers breaking their legs. They were using 20-lb. hammers. I could hear the bones crack. They'd holler some, and turn aside, but they didn't holler too loud. The guard, he was a pretty good piece off, and he couldn't hear them. They asked me to join them, but I said no.[48]

Governor Marvin Griffin ordered a full investigation, and the grand jury asked three men, Frank Bailey and C. A. Morton (both from Norcross) and J. Earle Simpson (of Buford), to investigate. Inexplicably, they filed a glowing report that contradicted the testimony of the guards and inmates, but the investigation brought increased scrutiny to the convict labor system that plagued the South throughout the nineteenth and twentieth century.[49]

The county also struggled with car thefts and the rise of "chop shops" as well as moonshine running, which contributed to the county's negative reputation. Wayne remembered, "In 1958, the county only had two deputy sheriffs and that made it difficult to be responsive to the public."[50] There were many who doubted their commitment to law and order. One story shows the depth of the problem. Daniel C. Cole, the sheriff from 1960 to 1963, in partnership with his deputies (Alex Evans and Thomas Ladford) and drivers (Harry Gravvit and M. C. Perry) were arrested on August 22, 1962. They had raided an illegal distillery, confiscated all the supplies, and then set up their own bootlegging operation in the barn of Horace J. Cover, another deputy.[51] A year later, Alex Evans was involved in the shooting of three officers who were investigating illegal activity on Beaver Ruin Road.[52]

Car thefts in the Atlanta metropolitan area were a major issue as well, and many of the cars stolen in the city ended up in chop shops in Gwinnett. The *Atlanta Constitution* reported that "in 1963, 3,417 Atlanta cars had been stolen, and by April first of 1964 there were already 1,078 taken with a total value of $1,448,800. That accounted for eighty five percent of the total crimes committed in the first quarter of 1964. Extending a monthly average, that year was on track to have 4,072 stolen. As a point of comparison, there were only 1,797 stolen cars reported in 1957."[53] The proliferation of chop shops in Gwinnett, where many of these stolen cars were torn apart for parts resale, further contributed to the county's reputation as a lawless land.

Another high-profile crime further cemented Gwinnett's reputation. Barbara Jane Mackle, a student at Emory University, was kidnapped by Gary Steven Krist and Ruth Eisenmann-Schier in 1968 and buried alive near Duluth. The ransom drama, eventual arrest of Krist and Eisenmann-Schier, and rescue of Barbara remained in the news and kept feeding into stereotypes about Gwinnett that would persist for another two decades.[54] One reason was that Gwinnett's historic conservative, segregationist past was slow to evolve. An unfortunate scandal erupted on March 6, 1978, when white supremacist Joseph Paul Franklin shot Larry Flynt, the publisher of *Hustler* magazine, and his lawyer, Gene Reeves, as they were leaving V&J Cafeteria in

Lawrenceville. Franklin was provoked by the publication of a photograph of an interracial couple. Flynt and Reeves were returning to the Gwinnett County Courthouse for the continuation of Flynt's obscenity trial.[55]

Against the backdrop of these scandals, leaders like Jimmy and Wayne Mason were "installing a formidable infrastructure, embracing conservative economic policies, attracting big businesses through creative tax policies, developing neighborhoods for families, and establishing an award-winning school district."[56] Their persistence would make all the difference.

# Chapter 3

## Laying the Groundwork

"I've been in every kind of business you can think of. You name it, I've been in it." —Wayne Mason

In 1947, two years after the end of World War II, the Georgia General Assembly established the Metropolitan Planning Commission (MPC), signaling the growing importance of coordinating the region's growth. The MPC was the first publicly supported, multi-county planning agency in the US, and its goal was to create the first master plan for the area, which at the time was only comprised of the City of Atlanta and Fulton and DeKalb Counties.[1] But that was soon to change. Thirteen years later, the MPC was replaced by the Atlanta Region Metropolitan Planning Commission, which expanded the boundaries to include Clayton, Gwinnett, and Cobb Counties. In 1971, the General Assembly chartered the Atlanta Regional Commission (ARC) with the support of then state representative Jimmy Mason, which included a thirty-nine-member board of elected officials and private citizens and a member of the Georgia Department of Community Affairs. The county chairperson served on the ARC, as did a mayor from each county. Gwinnett was well represented in the ARC, and Wayne Mason served on the board from 1977 to 1980.[2]

Reflecting on the post-war growth, historian Edward Hatfield explains,

> Atlanta's northern suburbs grew by leaps and bounds in the decades after World War II, but Gwinnett's rates of growth lagged behind metropolitan averages throughout the 1950s and 1960s, often by a wide margin. As local officials would later admit, the county's progress was initially stymied by a well-earned reputation for lawlessness and official indifference. It was an open secret that Gwinnett's farmers supplemented their income by bootlegging, for example, but when federal agents were called to investigate the practice in 1963, they were surprised to discover that local lawmen, including the county sheriff, were among the worst offenders.[3]

It would take some significant changes to shift the county's trajectory, a fact not lost on the rest of the state.

## From Three to Five

Corruption is one of the reasons that, in 1968, the Georgia General Assembly, in a bill authored by Jimmy Mason, expanded the Gwinnett County Commission from three to five seats and professionalized the administrative system. After this decision, "a new police chief was hired, the county's notorious prison system underwent real reform, and the new commissioners approved a bevy of reforms that ranged from land use planning to leash laws."[4] The change was prompted, in part, by a 1963 study commissioned by the University of Georgia's Institute of Law and Government. Prior to the change, commissioners were elected county-wide and paid $6,000 a year. As Elliott Brack argues, "In effect, what Gwinnett had was three lone individuals, each with the same authority. Things did not always operate smoothly. If you could get another commissioner to go along with you, things got done. If not, your efforts on the commission fell by the wayside. It wasn't always pretty."[5] Adding to the problems, most of the commissioners were elected from the larger cities of Lawrenceville or Buford, leaving the more rural parts of the county underrepresented and disempowered.

Changing the size of the commission required a constitutional amendment, and two state representatives from the county, Norris Nash and Jimmy Mason, along with district senator Earl Story, had to propose legislation to make the change. After maneuvering for some time, a provision was added to the November 1966 ballot, which failed by a vote of 5,054 to 5,383. The sticking point seemed to be the addition of hiring a county manager, rather than the plan to increase the commission's size from three to five members. A second referendum was put to the voters on April 10, 1968, with the sole focus of increasing the commission membership. Four of the members would run in districts, and the chairperson would be voted on by the entire county. The goal was to hire a full-time chairman who would be paid $15,000. The rest of the board would have staggered four-year terms, which meant that two or three seats would be up in each election cycle. This would help prevent a single commissioner from gaining too much power. The vote passed with an overwhelming majority, and in the fall of 1968, Gwinnett residents were given the opportunity to vote to fill five vacant positions. The new commission took office on January 1, 1969, with former commission member

W. R. "Dudge" Pruitt of Buford as chairman, supported by Carvis P. Williams of Snellville, Maron Buice of Sugar Hill, Julian Archer from Harbins, and Ray Gunnin of Norcross.[6] Wayne ran for a seat on the commission but lost to his cousin Carvis Williams.

The change in the composition of the county commission was of monumental importance to the future of the county. As Wayne explained,

> Before we went to a five-person commission, the county power structure was pretty corrupt. The Buford court system was just one example. They just about controlled everything in the county—including the lawyers and the politicians. Every elected official was beholden to them. There were gamblers and criminals, and even an incident where policemen were killed. Buford is still a force in the county, but nothing like what it used to be because the new commission structure distributed the power in the county.[7]

The newly seated commission was quick to act on Gwinnett's reputation for corruption. On March 8, Police Chief Harvard Norred announced his resignation, and the commission hired John Cunkleton, who promptly fired the entire staff. Two were eventually rehired (record keeper Gordon Parker and radio dispatcher Charles Sorrels), and thirty-two additional job searches were launched. Each new employee had to undergo a background check and engage in new, rigorous training programs. The commission also sought to reform the prison system, inspired by two reports, one by Joseph E. Ragen, an Illinois state warden, and the other by Dr. Frank L. Gibson at the University of Georgia.

Targeting Buford prison, the commission advocated a new focus on education and reform.[8]

These changes were not unique to Gwinnett, but common in the American South, as historian Joe Crespino argues in his book *In Search of Another Country: Mississippi and the Conservative Counterrevolution.*[9] The "Southern Strategy" advanced by Richard Nixon and the 1968 Republican Party platform squarely focused on anxiety about crime, lawlessness, and national security. At the 1968 convention, the platform was clearly articulated:

> Republicans believe that respect for the law is the cornerstone of a free and well-ordered society. We pledge vigorous and even-handed administration of justice and enforcement of the law. We must re-establish the principle that men are accountable for what they do, that criminals are responsible for their crimes, that while the youth's environment may help to explain the man's crime, it does not excuse that crime.[10]

Determined to turn the page on the county's past, the Republican platform gained traction, even among those who did not vote Republican. It was time for a new era, and supporting law and order and investing in infrastructure became the order of the day.

After 1972, the Gwinnett County Commission began to adopt modern management practices that would set the stage for growth over the next fifty years, and which they accomplished by developing a data collection system, hiring a county engineer, creating a land use plan, modernizing garbage collection, developing leash laws, reforming the issuance of business licenses, creating an efficient water and sewage system, developing a countywide fire, ambulance, and recreation system, and implementing a progressive financing system.[11] The key to making all of these changes was having the right team in place. In addition to the commissioners, the hiring of Wayne Shackelford on January 1, 1973, was critical. As a newly elected member of the commission, Wayne Mason was one of his most vocal supporters. Having formerly worked as a county extension agent, Shackelford knew Gwinnett and became known as "Mr. Inside."

The new county structure did more than change daily governance, it also positioned Gwinnett as a major player in the metropolitan region. Journalist Elliott Brack argues,

> Before 1950, Gwinnett citizens never considered themselves as part of the Metro Atlanta area. After all, going to Atlanta was difficult on two-lane roads. Telephoning Atlanta meant a long distance charge. Not only that, but the county was virtually all rural, sprinkled with several small cities, none over 4,000 population. Even Gwinnett cities were considered a great distance from one another, and a trip to the courthouse in Lawrenceville not only took people from the corners nearly an hour, but was a major trip.[12]

But on October 2, 1960, Norcross, Duluth, and Stone Mountain became part of the metropolitan Atlanta telephone service. Soon, Buford and Lawrenceville were added. The US Census Bureau added Gwinnett to the metro area in 1958, "when the area was expanded to five counties," and the completion of Interstate 85 through the county in 1967 and Interstate 285 in 1969 solidified Gwinnett's place in the metro region.[13] Brack observes, "For a few years, in the late 1950s and 1960s, Gwinnett was quietly growing. Up until about 1970, the rest of Metro Atlanta paid very little attention to Gwinnett County. People drove through the county on the way to Athens, or Greenville or Charlotte, but seldom noticed what was happening."[14]

## The Road to Progress

Metropolitan Atlanta started seeing growth in transportation in the 1940s, with an acceleration after the passage of the National System of Interstate and Defense Highways of 1956 (commonly referred to as the Interstate Act), during Dwight D. Eisenhower's presidency. Inspired by Germany's autobahn, Eisenhower discussed the plan in his State of Union address, explaining that the country was ready for a grand transportation plan:

> Legislation to provide a modern, interstate highway system is even more urgent this year than last, for 12 months have now passed in which we have fallen further behind in road construction needed for the personal safety, the general prosperity, [and] the national security of the American people.... I urged that measures be taken to complete the vital 40,000 mile interstate system over a period of 10 years at an estimated Federal cost of approximately 25 billion dollars.[15]

Construction of Gwinnett County's portion of the interstate had three possible paths: following US 23 through Gainesville, US 29 through Athens, or a direct path between Atlanta and Greenville, South Carolina. Georgia governor Ernest Vandiver advocated for the direct path that would go through his hometown with a promise that Interstate 985 (Sydney Lanier Parkway) would be built to accommodate Gainesville and that State Route 316 (University Highway) would become a controlled access road to Athens.[16] Interstate I-85 was constructed in five segments, and as Katheryn Nikolich explains,

> as each section was completed, the wooded ends provided excellent cover for the county's lawless reputation. Chop shop criminals and bootleggers used the unfinished roads as an easy access between Atlanta and Gwinnett County. The woods at the end of the highway afforded ample coverage, and the interstate offered direct service for stolen cars. The road slowly developed northeast from Atlanta toward South Carolina with stops at Jimmy Carter Boulevard, Beaver Ruin Road, Pleasant Hill Road, and Old Peachtree Road. The final leg through Gwinnett County was not completed until 1967.[17]

As Edward Hatfield argues, "The interstate's arrival had only a limited impact at first, as it may have deepened the county's association with criminality, as chop shops were reported to have proliferated under cover of nearby woods. Still, local officials remained convinced that the road was the 'key' to future growth."[18] Businesses soon followed, and county leaders helped bring Western Electric and distribution and warehousing firms to develop or settle in Gwinnett along with the development of Technology/Park Atlanta. Hatfield explains, "With the commitment to good schools, and an expanding commercial base that obviated the need for significant taxes on residential property, the county would become a preferred destination for Sunbelt migration, welcoming hundreds of thousands of white, middle-class newcomers through the 1970s and 1980s." In 1985, the Census Bureau reported that Gwinnett was the "fastest-growing county in the entire country."[19] In the 1970s and 1980s, growth topped 8 percent, prompting Lillian Webb to quip, "Sometimes I think all 230,000 of us are on Jimmy Carter Boulevard at the same time."[20]

As the county grew, so did the Masons' impact and influence. If you had to point to a turning point for the Mason brothers, it would be 1959. After high school, Jimmy joined Sears, Roebuck and Co. on Ponce de Leon Avenue (which was later redeveloped into Ponce City Market). He would later go on to work for Southern Bell as a cable splicer's helper. Jimmy married Helen Elizabeth Phillips on August 3, 1956, volunteered for the army, and was sent to Korea until 1959. Jimmy and Helen would later have three girls—Tracey, Teresa, and Tina.

In contrast to his brother, Wayne explained, "I didn't join any organization, even the Boy Scouts, who wear uniforms. I was too young for Korea and too old for Vietnam."[21] On September 5, 1959, he married Ann Biggers, and by the time he was twenty-six, they had four children—Keith, Kim, Kay, and Kristy.[22] Wayne continued to work at Goodyear until 1961. But the brothers both knew that this would be temporary, because they planned to build residential housing. They had formed the Mason Brothers Construction Company just at the right moment to capitalize on the baby boomers who saw suburban Gwinnett as a great place to live. But without much capital, they had to work full-time jobs while starting their construction business. Wayne started building houses, and Jimmy joined him full time in 1963, when he gave up his job selling Yellow Page advertising. Wayne explained, "Jimmy stayed until we made enough in the company to support both families. Whatever Jimmy's salary was at Southern Bell was the amount I took from the company. We shared everything 50-50."[23]

The brothers bought their first property from Harvie Ewing Jr., Jimmy's brother-in-law, in 1959 on Lanier Mountain. They had an unusual arrangement, as Wayne explained: "We would buy the lot, and Harvie would give us a deed for the lot. Harvie didn't require us to pay him until we sold the house, so that deed was worth gold to us. We would take that deed to the bank and borrow money to build the house."[24] Ewing played an outsized role in their early success, and Wayne remembered calling him "Moneybags" for his unwavering support. Ewing called Wayne "Fireball," a nickname that captured Wayne's energy and spirit. Soon, the brothers were making enough money to be self-sufficient. Their success in residential real estate echoed the broader transformation of the metro Atlanta region and throughout the Sunbelt. They helped contribute to the meteoric growth in housing in the 1960s and 1970s in Gwinnett County. The brothers' complementary skills helped the business thrive, as Elliott Brack argues: "Wayne usually was the lead with the decisions while Jimmy went along."[25] Primarily focused on Snellville, the Masons built their residential real estate company and managed to construct 1,800 single family houses between 1959 and 1972. One of Wayne's most vivid memories from this era came on November 22, 1963, right before Thanksgiving. When working on a house in Vinings, Wayne remembered, "We were pouring concrete on the driveway, and we heard the news that Kennedy had been killed on the radio. I was working with an African American man on the job, and I remember him saying of the assassination, 'Every time we get a good man, someone kills him.'"[26]

Richard Tucker, who worked for and with the Masons for decades, remembers this time:

> Wayne and Jimmy gave me my first job out of college in 1972. I graduated from UGA in the spring and started working for them. It was a great opportunity because they were building single-family homes at a time of real growth. I grew up in Stone Mountain, and my Dad's best friend was Wayne's uncle. As I was finishing school, they cooked up an idea that I would go work for the Masons. Jobs were not paying well, even at places like Coca-Cola and C & S Bank. I started with them and made five times what I would have at a more traditional entry-level position. The houses were not expensive but were good quality, and most of the clients were blue collar workers. Gwinnett was still pretty rural and undeveloped; I think there were only 10,000 non-agricultural jobs in the whole county when I started. It was a huge county, but the infrastructure just was not there. Wayne ran for county commission to help change things. He had a huge influence because he knew how to get things done. Before Wayne and the commission tackled the water issue, Gwinnett had to create inter-county agreements to keep the water and sewers working. Gwinnett would not be what it is today without Wayne and Jimmy. It would have grown, but not like it has. Cobb and Gwinnett counties mirror each other. Cobb was ten years

ahead of Gwinnett, but Gwinnett caught up and surpassed Cobb.[27]

## Housing the County

Growth in Gwinnett was inevitable, and many leaders saw the county's potential and expected it to double in size from the 1960s to the 1980s. The US Census, which first included Gwinnett in the Metropolitan Statistical Area in 1960, reported that Gwinnett's population in 1970 was 72,349; thirteen years later, it had more than doubled to 208,337 (an 188 percent increase).[28] Housing and building a strong infrastructure to accommodate growth was an essential part of Gwinnett's success. The median home value in the United States in 1940, on the eve of the US entry into World War II, was $2,938. By 1950, prices had jumped to $7,354, and then to $11,900 by 1960, a year after the Masons started building.[29] In 1959, when the Masons started selling homes, the asking prices were between $11,750 and $12,250. By 1972, prices had risen to between $13,000 to $15,000. With the Masons, buyers got a 1,526-square-foot house with a double carport. Wayne explained, "That's less than $100 a square foot. And they were good homes. Even if a buyer didn't add on to them, these same homes were reselling for $170,000 in 2008."[30] In 1972, the Masons' company built 565 homes. Wayne remembered fondly, "We made $176,000 in 1972. But you have to put in a lot of work to make that kind of money. Meanwhile, we were buying and selling land, and would have made more off the land than building the house. But we had other businesses."[31]

But the real estate business had boom and bust cycles, as Richard Tucker came to realize:

> I started with the Masons in 1972, and by 1976, the real estate market crashed. I had a young family, house, and had to scramble to make a living. I lived by a high school and went to ask the principal if they had a job for a teacher or coach. I had a degree in business and got a provisional certificate to teach at Loganville High School and coach football. In the spring of my second year, Jimmy came to see me to see if I wanted to come back and work with them. Wayne was now chairing the Gwinnett County Commission, and I went to work for the county administrator, Wayne Shackelford, in August 1977. I was his second in command and stayed there for three years. Then Virgil Williams, who had recently bought Gwinnett County Bank and Fulton County Bank, which merged into Heritage Bank [later Bank of America], gave me a job at the bank and at Williams Contracting. I did real estate on the side. Wayne and Jimmy taught me to be entrepreneurial and try new things to learn new skills.[32]

Understanding the power of diversification, Wayne and Jimmy also operated Mason Brothers Ceramic Tile and Suburban Realty and were partners in three funeral homes. The brothers partnered with Jimmy's brother-in-law Edgar Couch to create Couch and Mason Funeral Homes. Their other main company, Three M Investments, owned 700 acres of land that would become Summit Chase Country Club. Wayne recalled, "That was our first million-dollar deal. There were three of us in the deal, including our uncle Hilliard (Hill) Moore, who was in the auto business. We had purchased the land by advertising 'We Buy Land for Cash: Give Boot, Take Boot, Trade Even.'" The timing was just right, as Wayne explained: "In the 1960s and

1970s, people had quit farming, and there was a lot of land available. I remembered that in that early deal that we bought at least three other farms and then sold it to developers who wanted to build a golf course."[33]

There was no secret formula to the Masons' success: they worked hard, dealt honestly, and looked for strategic partnerships. As Richard Tucker once noted, "The great thing about Wayne [is that] he's always been willing to share the wealth, so to speak. He's always looking for partners, looking for opportunities for others. Just a really good businessperson and a civic-minded individual."[34] After leaving banking, Tucker came back to work with the Masons:

> My children were in middle school, and after years in banking and mortgage lending, I was ready to go back out on my own. One Friday, I left my job and used the weekend to set up my home office. I got business cards, and on Monday morning, I started calling everyone I knew to drum up mortgage business. I took a break to run into Snellville to get some lunch and saw Jimmy. He invited me to come to the old Gwinnett Federal Building and told me to use his office. I worked at home for half a day before I was back in business with the Masons. Jimmy had been in the liquor business. He had two stores, and I bought one in June 1990. Then we bought another, I ended up running five stores for thirty years. Six years later, I became the chief operating officer of the Gwinnett Chamber of Commerce, where I stayed for seven years. In 2003, Bartow Morgan Jr., Wayne, and I started a business, Arlington Capital, a company still in business.[35]

Richard Tucker's assessment of his career speaks directly to the Mason's influence:

I could have ended up anywhere within 100 miles of here. I would be the same person, with the same work ethic, the same drive, but the opportunity would not have been there. That was because of the Masons. Gwinnett presented an amazing opportunity to build something big, and relationships mattered. Without the Masons, I would have done okay, but I know I would not have been as successful as I am. Everybody knew the Masons. They were major players in so many arenas. Everybody knew them as friends, partners, and even rivals. Even if you didn't agree with them, you respected them.[36]

# Chapter 4

# Servant Leadership

> "If it was for the benefit of the county, we would find a way to do it."—Wayne Mason

While the Masons were growing their businesses, they also followed in the footsteps of their family in turning to public service. As active business leaders in the community, they realized that the county was not progressing as effectively as its more prosperous neighbors. Jimmy's and Wayne's foray into politics was not self-serving. According to *Gwinnett Magazine*, "In their aspirations, the brothers had something in common: they wanted to see Gwinnett County keep getting better and better. Both used their positions as a means to do just that. For Wayne, seeing the county get decent water and sewer service was the very reason he ran for commissioner in the first place."[1]

## A Statewide Strategy

Jimmy Mason paved the way for the brothers' entry into politics. He was elected to three terms on the Snellville City Council, serving from 1961 to 1966. Then he ran for state legislator in 1966, where he remained for eight years, until 1974. In 1968, Jimmy had a chance meeting with Sam Nunn at the Beacon Hotel in Daytona Beach that would help reshape Georgia politics. As Peter Kent explains, "After the 1970 census, Mr. Mason worked on remapping the legislative districts. He proposed a congressional district for Middle Georgia that would give Mr. Nunn a seat to run for. The proposal lost by one vote. The defeat led to Mr. Nunn running for the U.S. Senate."[2] Serving from 1972 to 1997, Nunn would remain one of the most influential senators in this era.

Jimmy's personality suited politics because he was outgoing and built a robust network at the state level. While in the Georgia General Assembly, he served with his cousin Norris Nash from 1967 to 1971, and they worked together to pass legislation that helped Gwinnett County, notably creating the Public Facilities Authority, the Recreation Authority, and the Water and Sewer Authority.[3] Their careful attention to building infrastructure has continued to pay long-term dividends. Wayne explained,

> Authorities were the only way to finance these big-dollar, long-range improvements. After all, the county commission didn't have much revenue then. We were operating the entire county on a budget of less than $7 million in those days. We would not have the water and sewer system today, which has been the backbone of our growth, without authority financing. I served myself for most of my term as a commissioner, until 1980, as chair of the Water and Sewer Authority, because I understood finance. You must realize that Jimmy and I had a bigger budget in those days than the county had.[4]

Reflecting on Jimmy's impact, Peter Kent, writing his obituary for the *Atlanta Journal*, declared, "During his four terms in the House, [Jimmy] Mason sponsored legislation that revamped Gwinnett government, preparing the county for its transition from its rural past to a booming metropolitan community.[5] He also helped develop Highway 78, which brought development to the southern end of the county.

As a longtime friend of the Masons, Richard Tucker shared that "Jimmy was very effective in the state legislature. He got things done quietly, not caring who got the credit. He worked behind the scenes and built relationships, especially those with Sam Nunn and Zell Miller. If not for Jimmy, I'm not sure the Masons would have been as successful in the public arena."[6] Sam Williams, the former chief operating officer of the Metropolitan Atlanta Chamber of Commerce, knew Jimmy by reputation and recalled his nickname "Diamond Jim."[7]

For seventeen years, Jimmy was on the Georgia State Properties Commission (from 1975 to 1992), which bought land for governmental purposes, and in July 1992 was named to the board of directors for the Georgia Ports Authority (GPA). Wayne explained his brother's contribution to the GPA: "Under Governor Zell Miller, Georgia really poured money into developing and modernizing the state's ports. Jimmy traveled all over the world looking at other ports to see how they operated. Jimmy took that work very seriously." He was on a GPA trip in May 1998 when he was injured in an accident from which complications arose that cost Jimmy his life.[8] Jimmy's life and work have been recognized in numerous ways. In 1998, the Georgia General Assembly passed a resolution noting his accomplishments. In 1999, a junction at GA 124 and US 78 was named for Jimmy, and in 2001 Governor Roy Barnes dedicated the Ports Authority rail transfer facility after Jimmy on the day Keith Mason became the GPA chair. As Jimmy's daughter, Tracey Mason, recalled, "When the junction was named for my father, I had a chance to thank the legislature and laughed as I recalled my father told my cousin, Pamela Ewing, that there was a world beyond where Highway 78 met Highway 124. So, it was ironic that they named it for him."[9]

The Mason Mega Rail, which was completed at the Port of Savannah, "is the largest one-terminal dock intermodal facility in North America [featuring] more than 120,000 feet of rail and 18 working tracks, capable of serving six 10,000-foot trains simultaneously with 10 new rail-mounted gantry cranes."[10] It is a fitting tribute to a man who contributed so much to the Port Authority's growth more than a generation ago.

## Building the Infrastructure

Wayne Mason's political career began in 1968 when he unsuccessfully ran for the Gwinnett Board of Commissioners. Wayne recalled, "I first ran for the district commission seat in 1968 and got beat by Carvis Williams, my cousin, by 455 votes. I lost in my home precinct in Snellville by 228 votes. Hugh Snell liked to tell people that Carvis took two bushels of peas and beat me."[11] Wayne ran a progressive, even modern campaign, explaining, "I spent $7,800 and had all types of items, from hats, bumper stickers, balloons, even put out a newspaper, and still lost. But if I had won that Snellville precinct, I would have won the election. I was 28 years old then, and people just thought I was too young to be a commissioner."[12]

Four years later, Wayne's luck had changed and, at the age of thirty-two, he was elected to the Gwinnett Board of Commissioners. The night after the election was more memorable than his victory. Wayne, Jimmy, Norris Nash, Warren Bush, Larry Smith, Doug McCurdy, and Hill Moore were playing a friendly poker game. Wayne remembered,

> Back in the 1970s, it was common knowledge that a bunch of us played poker every week, usually on Wednesday night, and often on Saturday afternoon. I had 700 acres off U.S. Highway 78 between Loganville and Snellville, which would later become Summit Chase Country Club. There was a boat house on J. B. Johnson Lake in the middle of those 700 acres where we played.[13]

At around 10:30 P.M. on August 9, 1972, the *Atlanta Journal* reported a group of masked men "broke in on the weekly poker game of a group of Gwinnett businessmen and politicians last Wednesday and seriously injured contractor Warren A. Bush of Lithonia with a shotgun blast in the shoulder." Wayne recalled,

> Three guys in masks blew out the window with a shotgun. The blasts went past my left ear. I could hear it go by. Three people blasted through a glass door, came in wearing masks, and told the players to get on the floor. They scooped up the cash on the table, later estimated at $1,500. They also demanded rings, credit cards, and each person's cash. Included in the haul were some campaign checks, estimated at about $12,000, that [I] had in my wallet, and had not deposited.[14]

Jimmy remembered, "They appeared real unhappy that there wasn't much money there."[15] He would later joke about the robbers, "They held the best hand, so I folded."[16] The thieves were eventually arrested, and Wayne remembers that he and his friends had to go to superior court, where they pled "no contest" for violating state gambling laws and each paid a $1,000 fine.

Despite this inauspicious beginning to his political career, Wayne would serve and lead the county at a critical period in its history, from 1972 to 1980, serving as commission chair from 1976 to 1980. Wayne and the rest of the commissioners did not have delusions of grandeur; they just wanted to solve problems that affected their neighbors every single day. Water was at the top of the list. As Wayne explained, "In the southern part of the county, if you wanted to take a shower, you had to get up at five or six in the morning. If not, there was no water pressure, and you were out of luck. Then the whole cycle started again in the afternoon. If you wanted to do laundry or water your garden, you had to do it late at night. It was crazy."[17]

Wayne was good at forecasting,

> We knew growth was coming. To finance the water and sewer bonds, we structured the authorities so they could borrow money on an anticipated revenue bond based on the future growth. We borrowed the money for the Lake Lanier water plant, capitalized the interest for three years, and then went to full cash with interest for another three years. We backloaded the bonds, paying interest-only in the early years and principal in the last years. Think what a dollar was worth in 1973 compared to what it was worth 25 years later. That way you could make the numbers

> dance. Everything was done based on the growth that we knew was coming. Without the growth in Gwinnett and without the balance between commercial and residential development in the Gwinnett tax digest, we would not have had the first-class water and sewer system or top-notch schools we have today.[18]

Wayne also recalled, "There were a few families that, basically, owned the biggest part of land in the county. And between these families, you'd have marrying back and forth. When I started out, I couldn't hardly run a waterline or grade a road that didn't cross the property of somebody who was kin to me or who had married into the family."[19]

Wayne Shackelford, who served as Gwinnett County's administrator and later commissioner of the Georgia Department of Transportation, played an equally critical role in the transformation. He understood the power of reliable water and sewers. He explained that the authorities "under Georgia law are created for one reason, to defeat the Georgia Constitution. The Georgia Constitution says you got to pay your debts each and every time by the end of the year, or you can't borrow a dime the next year. You create an authority. It can enter into long-term debt, but it's got to have a source of repayment, so you contract between the authority and the general government to assure those payments."[20] Sam Williams explained,

> The Masons understood infrastructure and were instrumental in the issue of water governance and management. They helped build a sewage treatment plant that discharged drinkable water. It was the biggest and cleanest in the state and was a good example for

> other counties. They were some of the first developers to see that you had to figure out water and sewer for the whole region before building anything. Most developers fail to look beyond the boundaries of the land they own. Not the Masons. They understood that you had to look at water, sewer, transportation, schools, business development and housing all at the same time. They also saw the importance of attracting new residents, including immigrants, to the region. They were not mired in the segregationist politics of the past, but saw what was good for business and the future.[21]

Wayne would go on to explain, "We really cared about doing right by the county and saw that segregation was both wrong and bad for business. I was raised in the South and saw plenty of friends and colleagues get tangled up in racism. Attracting diverse residents to the county was a good thing and helps explain why Atlanta is bigger than Birmingham or Memphis. It's because we didn't get tangled up in all that nonsense."[22]

## The Power of Water

Growth would be driven by water. As the county's website reported, "For three consecutive years, 1986 through 1988, Gwinnett ranked as the fastest growing county in the U.S. among counties with a population greater than 100,000."[23] That kind of growth was not possible without a reliable water and sewer system, and the infrastructure set in the 1970s and early 1980s made it all possible. Two things made this work: getting support from the Georgia General Assembly to establish a water and sewer authority and receiving permission to pull water from Lake Lanier from the US Army

Corps of Engineers.[24] It helped that Jimmy was in the state legislature, lobbying hard for Gwinnett's future. His daughter, Tracey Mason, says of both Wayne and Jimmy that they were "the right people at the right time with the right skills. When you put the two of them in a room there was nothing they couldn't get accomplished. Whenever I used to ask them how they were able to achieve all they did, they just told me, 'nobody ever told us we couldn't, so we just did it.'"[25]

Getting water from Lake Lanier was no easy feat, but Wayne had a plan, as he explained: "There was a guy who was a retired colonel in the Army, Harold Dye [who ran for mayor of Atlanta in 1973]. He knew someone who ran the Corps of Engineers out of Mobile. I talked to Dye and said 'Harold, what would you charge us to help us get a permit?' He said, '$15,000.' I put him on my plane, sent him to Mobile, and we got a permit."[26] The permit turned out to be the easy part. Mason explained that he received some pushback from Republicans in DeKalb County.

> They all pitched a fit over it. So, Bo Calloway, Secretary of the Army who was over the Corps of Engineers, called me up and said 'Mason, what sized plant are you building up there?' And, I said, 'Well, we planned for first phase to be permitted at 240 million gallons.' He said, 'I'm taking a lot of heat off the Republicans about that permit. If I cut it back to 40 million gallons, will that be alright?' I said, 'Do whatever you have to do. We'll increase it later.' So, they cut it to 40 million gallons because that sounded like a lot of water then. But [that] got us that permit.[27]

Jim Henderson reflected on the significance of this achievement:

> The county we know today would not exist but for Wayne's work on water. I remember when all these negotiations were happening, and the engineers were talking about what they could and could not do. At the time, the county had a small intake facility and plant on the Chattahoochee River in Duluth below the dam. There were discussions about building a facility on Lake Lanier to increase capacity. But the engineers were skeptical because they knew they had to convince the Army Corps of Engineers. No one thought it was possible, but Wayne got it done. I don't know anybody else who could have achieved that feat. Today, with all the litigation about water, it would be nearly impossible.[28]

As Wayne later explained, "I knew that whoever controlled water controlled the destiny of the whole area. We knew what level to take the water at where it'd be pure enough to shoot in your veins."[29] Ultimately Gwinnett was given permission to remove 200 million gallons per day and later borrowed $44 million in water and sewer bonds to upgrade the system. *Gwinnett Magazine* reported, "The system, to this day, is one of the best in the world, according to some reports—pulling and cleaning water from the lake; returning wastewater to streams even cleaner than it was when taken from Lake Lanier."[30]

Developing a countywide sewer system was also a game changer. Early sewer plants in Gwinnett were often built for subdivisions and were private systems. As Elliott Brack states, "It wasn't until Gwinnett County started considering collecting sewage from a wider watershed that more modern and larger plants were built."[31] The Gwinnett County Water and Sewer Authority was established in 1970, which spurred construction throughout the county. The Crooked Creek Water Reclamation Plant was built in 1972 in Peachtree Corners, and a year later, the Jackson Creek Plant opened. In 1978, the Beaver Ruin plant began operation. That next year, the Yellow River Plant was constructed in Lilburn in what would be the largest water basin in Gwinnett. That plant was followed by the F. Wayne Hill Water Resource Center in the 1990s, which boasted the most modern filtration system in the county.[32]

## Small Changes, Big Impact

Another major innovation was developing a countywide business license system in Gwinnett. Before Wayne's tenure on the commission, companies that wanted to do business in the county had to buy individual licenses in different cities. As Wayne explained,

> companies should not have to buy ten to twelve different licenses to do business in the county. It did not make sense. So, we came up with a plan that if you bought a business license in Snellville, it had reciprocity with other cities in Gwinnett. It made it so much easier to do business, and all the money went into one big pot. Then the commission divided the funds among cities based on population. We did something similar with fire and ambulance services. Instead of having one for each city, we developed county-wide systems. That way nobody was in competition with each other for emergency services. As a result, our fire rating was significantly less than neighboring Dekalb County.[33]

Developing a master plan for the county's recreation was also a priority in this period. In 1973, the Recreation Department argued that "the larger the county grows, the more its citizens will need and seek open space. Today's open space will be tomorrow's subdivision or shopping center if Gwinnett fails to acquire land now. The projected growth in the county indicates the need for planning, acquiring, and preserving open space today."[34] While it would take two more decades for the county to have the resources to purchase greenspaces, in 1975, the General Assembly allowed militia districts to join the recreation district. After various cities like Dacula and Suwanee joined, the county was able to adopt a countywide master plan in 1986. The next year, the Gwinnett County Parks and Recreation Department was given authority over the whole county, which led to a dramatic expansion of recreational activities.[35]

Taxes also became part of the commission's strategy, and they played a major role in helping support the county's public school system. In 1972, the county's first major industry, Western Electric, moved to Jimmy Carter Boulevard. It was quite a coup, and the commission helped develop a tax abatement called a "freeport tax" to seal the deal. As Katheryn Nikolich argues, "This innovative levy allowed companies to store their goods free of taxes until they were sold. The tax abatement, the proximity to railroad and interstate transportation, and the powerful combination of [Commission chairman W. R. Pruitt, Mason, and Shackelford convinced them to build their new complex in Gwinnett County."[36] As Wayne explained, "the plant could just have easily have been located one exit south in DeKalb County, and Gwinnett would still have to educate the children of the Western Electric workers."[37] The strategy paid off; Western Electric opened in 1972 to produce copper wiring for the telephone industry, and by the end of 1973 had 2,317 workers and paid the county it's first million-dollar ad valorem check. The county invested that money into education. Five years later, Western Electric was employing 3,800, and the county's reputation for being good for business had been cemented.[38]

But this approach was not without its challenges, and a problem emerged with Michelin Tire Company over the assessment of the ad valorem tax on inventory held at their warehouse from January 1, 1972, to January 1, 1973. Michelin contested the tax and turned to an 1872 Supreme Court ruling, *Low v. Austin*, which was a case involving French champagne that had long been on the books. The decision was based on the lower court's interpretation of whether imports were exempt if kept in the original packaging. Michelin argued that because it was a global company that warehoused goods in multiple states and imported products from overseas that they did not owe the tax. Gwinnett countered that the international inventory was mixed with the domestic stock and thus did not qualify for the exemption. Michelin ultimately took the case to the Georgia Supreme Court and the US Supreme Court, which ruled in the county's favor.[39] The complicated case and related litigation certainly cost Gwinnett, but the result solidified the commission's approach to attracting business.

Housing was an ongoing issue for the commission and remained so when Wayne was elected. As a developer, he had a unique perspective on the needs and challenges that the county faced. In 1972, the commission rejected proposals for five new subdivisions because of the inadequate water supply. Carvis Williams, one of the commissioners, explained, "Due to the overloading of our schools and until we get our water system straightened out, I would recommend we disapprove these."[40] The decision helped spur the commission to solve the water and sewer issues that were a barrier to growth.

The connection between housing and education might not be immediately obvious, but Wayne often argued that "the whole reason to draw new businesses to the county is to help pay for a good school system."[41] Gwinnett's schools developed along train corridors, and each cluster (Berkmar, Central Gwinnett, Dacula, Duluth, Norcross, North Gwinnett, and South Gwinnett) included a high school and multiple middle and elementary schools, depending on the population.[42] The growth in Gwinnett's schools, just like suburbanization of the county, is complicated and has its roots in the "white flight" of the 1960s and 1970s. With the passage of *Brown v. Board of Education* and the subsequent desegregation of public schools, many Southern communities saw white families leave urban centers for the suburbs. This was reflected by the Atlanta Board of Education's report of a 5,000-student drop in enrollment in 1974.[43]

Sensing an opportunity, Gwinnett leaders and the commission began investing in education and focusing on bringing in strong leadership. John William (J. W.) Benefield Jr. began his career in 1950 teaching agriculture to Bethesda and Central Gwinnett high school students in Lawrenceville. In 1961, he became assistant superintendent of Gwinnett County Schools and superintendent in 1967. Ten years later, he was named Outstanding Superintendent of 1977 by the Georgia Association of Education Leadership. Benefield was followed by Alton Crews (1977–1989), who worked hard to refocus the county curriculum on core courses. He sought to combat declining test scores, establish strong partnerships with local businesses and the Gwinnett Chamber of Commerce, and increase the budget, and he spearheaded the founding of Gwinnett Technical Institute in 1984.[44] He was largely successful, and the twenty-nine county schools in 1975 grew to fifty-nine schools by 1990.[45] Crews was followed by several leaders, the most significant of whom was Alvin Wilbanks (1996–2021). Wilbanks is largely credited with raising standardized test scores, building the school district's reputation, and promoting growth within the county. Wayne Mason recalled, "Alvin really understood what the schools needed. He attracted quality teachers and kept the politics out of it. He worked on developing STEM education. He really helped build one of the best school districts in the nation."[46] Wilbanks advised three Georgia governors and two US education secretaries on legislation and was a finalist in 2005 for national superintendent of the year. During his time as superintendent, Gwinnett won the Broad Prize for Urban Education twice, the only county in the nation to do so. After his contract was not renewed in 2021,[47] Wilbanks reflected, "I never forget who schools belong to. They don't belong to the board of education. They don't belong to the school administration. They belong to the people."[48]

## Good for the County

The decisions the Gwinnett Board of Commissioners made in the 1970s and 1980s transformed the county for generations to come. *Gwinnett Magazine* reported, "Over the next several years, Wayne and the commission worked to fund projects through the water and sewer authority, as well as a water intake for Lake Lanier, establishment of the public facilities authority, recreation authority, a uniform business license system and more. In short, they worked together to lay extensive infrastructural and procedural tracks to keep Gwinnett County going."[49] Wayne explained, "I had the confidence of the board. If we came up with something that was good for the county it was unanimous. Always unanimous.... I never served with a person on the board of commissioners who would put being elected over doing what was good for the county."[50] During Wayne's eight years on the commission, eight hundred miles of roads were paved and four hundred more were graded. Looking back and realizing how much growth was really coming, he said, "I would have built a lot more multilane roads."[51]

In describing his personal philosophy, Wayne said, "I never tried to have the limelight. Actions speak louder than words. Anybody can go out and blow their own horn, but people who were here know it. I spent all of my time on water, sewer and transportation, and finances of the county...[but] it was a combined effort from everybody to put Gwinnett on the map, and we did."[52] Reflecting on this time period, Wayne Shackelford explained, "The great leaders of the world don't make decisions based on the next vote. They make decisions in spite of the next vote. They make hard decisions.... Great leaders, great constitutional boards or statutory boards set policy and find the right leaders, and then the right leaders, with the confidence those men and women have, can then turn their dreams into reality."[53] Wayne Mason embodied these traits, as evidenced by his actions during his time on the county commission.

# Chapter 5

## A Rocky Road

> "You can try to keep up with Wayne Mason, but you'll fall behind."—*Gwinnett Magazine*, March 2022

Changes in banking regulations and a faltering economy brought serious challenges to the Mason brothers in the 1970s and 1980s. At one point, they were nearly bankrupt, however, they recovered their momentum, repaid debts, and returned to prosperity. They extended their businesses, made their first million-dollar deal—the sale of land that became Summit Chase Country Club in 1973—and built Snellville Plaza, bringing in the first chain grocery store that dramatically increased the value of the brothers' land holdings. By the late 1970s, Jimmy and Wayne owned all or a portion of 18,000 acres of land, and they saw Gwinnett County experience meteoric growth during this period—in the form of subdivisions, schools, interstates, warehouses, light industry, office parks, and high-tech headquarters. A shining achievement came on February 1, 1984, when more than "50,000 people converged on a site just north of Interstate 85 and Pleasant Hill Road to celebrate the opening of Gwinnett Place Mall."[1] But the county also struggled to manage the growth, and one main area of conflict was expanding mass transit.

The expansion of the Metropolitan Atlanta Rapid Transit Authority (MARTA) was a source of controversy during this period. Despite attempts to offer the county sensible transit solutions, residents routinely objected, citing an unproven but persistent theory that when rails come, crime follows. As Edward Hatfield explains,

> between 1971, when MARTA first appeared on county ballots, and 2019, when voters considered it for a third time, metropolitan Atlanta welcomed more than four million new residents and expanded its land area by a staggering 6,700 square miles—rates of growth that led urban redevelopment scholar Christopher Leinberger to speculate that it was "probably the fastest-growing of any metropolitan area in the history of the world."[2]

The rejection of MARTA in a county that desperately needed transportation solutions showed how "the Atlanta region became a national model for uneven development, political dysfunction, and the perils of automobility."[3]

Affordable and reliable transportation solutions were desperately needed because, throughout the 1970s and 1980s, the population of Gwinnett was regularly growing an average of 8 percent a year. In fact, historian Edward Hatfield argues that "no less than 70 percent of all growth occurred in Cobb and Gwinnett Counties, and by 1990, when MARTA appeared again on Gwinnett's ballots, a majority of jobs of every variety were located in the city's northern suburbs."[4] Both Gwinnett and Cobb had rejected MARTA expansion to their detriment. County boosters saw the problem: "Lower wage workers could not reach the bevy of jobs at Gwinnett Place and elsewhere without MARTA, and without an adequate labor supply, business would slow, tax receipts would dwindle, and area homeowners would be left to shoulder the difference."[5]

The county's resistance to adding mass transit revealed deep prejudices and was driven by vocal opponents. As Hatfield explains, "Anna Roupe knew exactly why MARTA wanted into Gwinnett County. It didn't have to do with travel times or metropolitan cooperation; neither did it have to do with curbing pollution, gas prices, or any other of the other reasons offered on the system's behalf. No, Roupe claimed, it was much more simple than all that. MARTA was 'broke and they need our money.'"[6] Roupe made opposing MARTA into a full-time job and was joined by a number of other groups. There was a great deal of fear that "MARTA wouldn't just provide locals with ready access to Atlanta; it would also bring Atlanta to them, a prospect that occasioned 'wild outbursts of racism and jingoism.'"[7] As Hatfield explains, "For too many of Gwinnett's voters, the equation was simple: rails would come, crime would follow, and Gwinnett would be transformed into a 'Belgian Congo.'"[8]

Wayne Mason explained the lost opportunity:

> MARTA would have improved our job base. Businesses only want to locate where they can hire people to work. We had great schools, and we needed reliable and affordable transportation. Not having MARTA meant we lost a lot of opportunity to DeKalb and Fulton Counties. Manufacturing businesses had very specific criteria for choosing a site, and public transportation was at the top of the list. We could not check that box in Gwinnett and we

> had to overcome that obstacle. I think it was short-sighted, but it's hard to change people's minds once they are made up.[9]

## The Changing Business Climate

In the 1970s, Gwinnett's business landscape started to change as well. Western Electric became the first major industry in Gwinnett, opening a facility near Jimmy Carter Boulevard and I-85, and "it brought about 2,500 jobs—jobs filled, in many instances, by well-paid Gwinnett newcomers (mostly white, but some black) who wanted good homes and good schools for their kids."[10] New construction, spurred on by the housing boom that the Masons started in 1959, also brought new workers, notably from Mexico and Central America. Wayne explained one of the reasons for Gwinnett's success:

> We understood the importance of diversification. We met with a lot of different people and countries, including the Japanese. They wanted to bring Panasonic to the county. We worked hard to make that happen and even allowed them to use the public schools on the weekends for language and culture classes. That also helped attract Korean companies. The secret was to be in a lot of different kinds of businesses. If you only had General Motors and they went on strike, you were in big trouble.[11]

The western edge of Norcross became a major area for growth in the early 1970s. Just as Western Electric was getting started, Peachtree Corners was developing into a desirable residential and commercial area. Technology Park Atlanta was established, and Electromagnetic Sciences (EMS) rented a 13,000-square-foot building. The company, an offshoot of Scientific-Atlanta, "facilitated communication between orbiting satellites by microwave transmission." Dr. John Pippin, the founder of Scientific-Atlanta and head of EMS, recalls, "When we contracted for our building, we were the first company to locate there. We crossed farmland to get to the site, and sometimes left gates open and let cows out of their pasture before we realized it."[12] He also recalled having to pay extra delivery fees because companies thought Gwinnett was too far from downtown Atlanta. EMS was joined by the Institute of Industrial Engineers and other companies who found appealing both the parkland setting as well as easy access to Peachtree Industrial Boulevard. The development soon ran out of land, and in 1982, Technology Park Atlanta purchased 1,626 acres of land in Johns Creek on Highway 141 near the Forsyth-Fulton County boundary. Eventually, 2.8 million square feet of space was developed there.[13] The growth would only continue, Elliott Brack observes: "In the mid-1970s, a scientific development was about to explode which would dramatically change the world, and, in Gwinnett County, would solidify the position of Peachtree Corners as the key location for high technology firms within Metro Atlanta for the next decade."[14] Companies such as Hayes Microcomputers would help solidify Gwinnett's reputation as a hub for innovation.

As the county grew, so did the impact of the Masons. Building on their residential success, Jimmy and Wayne decided to move into commercial real estate. Snellville Plaza was one of the Masons' most important enterprises. They knew that all of those new residents needed places to shop.

So, this seemed like a logical next step. Snellville Plaza was developed at the intersection of Highway 78 and Georgia Highway 124 in downtown Snellville, and it brought the county's first chain grocery store, Winn-Dixie. Wayne recalled, "We signed a sweetheart contract that kept the rent one percent of gross sales. Getting that supermarket to come to Snellville, the first one here, increased the price of all my land by $100 a lot. And when you own 2,200 acres of land, you stand to make some real money. For without the convenience of the supermarket, land is worth nothing."[15] By 1972, their investments in land holdings really started to pay off. One of the largest was a 5,518-acre plot in Smithsonia (bridging Clarke, Wilkes, and Oglethorpe Counties). When they sold the land in 1976 for $2.8 million, they only owed $800,000.[16]

Understanding the range of enterprises the Masons were involved in explains many of their successes. They partnered with Edgar Couch on funeral homes in Lawrenceville, but Wayne never liked the business: "It bothered me, big time, for I did not like to make money on someone's miseries."[17] They also worked with J. Mack Robinson, one of the wealthiest business leaders in Georgia at the time, to start Gwinnett County Bank in 1969, located in Snellville. When Robinson, the majority owner, decided to leave the business, the Masons bought his share, but this brought new problems because the Federal Deposit Insurance Company (FDIC) refused to approve the transaction because they were engaged in litigation over Hamilton Bank in Chattanooga.[18] Ultimately, the Masons invited their cousin Virgil Williams to buy Robinson's shares and sold their own to him as well. Wayne recalled, "I called Virgil and showed him the figures on a Friday, and Monday he said he thought it was a good idea. We set him up with Mack Robinson, and he bought Mack's stock. We sold him our stock at the same price he paid Mack."[19] Williams would become very successful and played a role in helping promote developing banks in supermarkets in the Southeast. The Masons also invested in liquor stores with Roddy Sturdivant. Once Lilburn allowed bottled liquor to be sold in 1977, the Masons built a store on Indian Trail Road and expanded to Conyers, Suwanee, and Duluth.

Despite the county's proximity to Atlanta, Gwinnett was plagued by issues more akin to its rural counterparts. The area was underserved medically until the 1970s. This is long after major hospitals like Emory, Piedmont, Egleston, and Northside were operating in Atlanta. In Snellville,

> five different doctors practiced here at different times from 1885–1930. Most were bi-vocational, working as farmers or merchants, to supplement their incomes. The city was without physicians from then until 1956, when the extended community built a doctor's office and recruited a physician; two physicians practiced from the facility before it was sold. Dr. Edward Bowen came here in 1971 as a general practitioner and immediately began recruiting medical specialists and spearheading a campaign to build a hospital in the city. By the end of the 1970s, the city had attracted young specialists in cardiology, gynecology, pediatrics, urology, ENT, surgery, and other fields of specialization. Dentists Hugh and Anne Mazzawi arrived in 1969 and helped to recruit some of these new professionals. Gwinnett Community Hospital opened in 1980 with 103 beds (max).[20]

Wayne and Jimmy were instrumental in recruiting Dr. Edward Bowen to come to Snellville, and he recalled that "not only did it help the whole county. It also meant that my land just went up another $100 per lot. There's no telling what I made off that."[21] Jimmy Mason later served on the Gwinnett Hospital Authority Board and the Promina Gwinnett Health System Board in the 1980s and 1990s, providing the same kind of community leadership that Gwinnett needed.

The 1970s and 1980s presented a difficult economic situation not just for Gwinnett, but for the whole nation. The 1970s saw soaring energy prices, high interest rates, and growing unemployment. On NPR's *Weekend Edition*, Scott Horsley explained, "The 1970s were bookended by oil shocks that brought soaring prices for gasoline. Meat prices also spiked. On the popular sitcom *All in the Family*, Archie Bunker was reduced to eating meatless spaghetti."[22] The 1980s did not bring much relief. Writing for the *Bureau of Labor Statistics Monthly Labor Review*, Michael Urquhart and Marillyn Hewson argue that the 1981 to 1982 recession was the worst economic downturn in the United States since the Great Depression. Unemployment was widespread, and construction, manufacturing, and the auto industries were hard hit. Three-fourths of all job losses in the goods-producing sector were in manufacturing, and the residential construction industry and auto manufacturers ended the year with 22 percent and 24 percent unemployment, respectively.[23]

Wayne Mason recognized how these larger issues would bring additional complications for their businesses. "About that time I owned 18,000 acres of land, and I thought I was Rockefeller," he recalled, adding, "but shortly after that I was broke for all intents and purposes. Since 1959, I never experienced a shortage of money, just a shortage of collateral." What caused it? The recession of the 1970s and changes to banking rules made it hard to borrow money. As Wayne explained,

> We had a lot of non-earning assets, which were listed as liabilities, so they could not be listed by the banking rules on the asset side. It stopped our borrowing and forced us to sell land at a virtual liquidation. We sold land, then we had to take a mortgage back. We would service the first mortgage and take a second mortgage. But there was no way to immediately pay out the first or second. But we worked it off, though we lost a lot of money. We ended up paying everyone off. But then we came back ourselves.[24]

But this was also an exciting time for Gwinnett, and 1984 seems to have been a critical year for growth and change. Gwinnett Place Mall opened on February 1, 1984. Prior to that date, "Gwinnett had been the largest county in population east of the Mississippi without a mall of its own."[25] That same year, three hospitals (Button Gwinnett Hospital, Joan Glancy Hospital, and Buford Hospital) combined into the Lawrenceville Medical Center. They eventually opened the Summit Ridge Center for Psychiatry and Addiction Medicine in 1993, and Gwinnett Medical System opened a second hospital in Duluth in 2006. Under the guidance of Gwinnett superintendent Alton Crews, the county opened Gwinnett Tech in 1984. As Elliott Brack argues, "Launching its own technical school gave Gwinnett businesses an advantage by tailoring courses to local needs and producing graduates able to step directly into productive jobs with local employers."[26] The final major change in 1984 was the political shift from Democratic to Republican. That year, sixteen Gwinnett Republicans all won their elections; only Democrat Alton Tucker—longtime friend—a probate judge who faced no opposition, remained in power.[27]

## The End of an Era

In 1988, Jimmy made the decision to step back from their various businesses. As Wayne remembered, "We were close as brothers, and we split everything as partners, fifty-fifty. He was, as my mother, Ida Belle, told me, always searching for the twin brother who died at birth. But we worked well together."[28] Wayne also recalled, "He let me take the lead in deals, and didn't pay all that much attention to details. One time, when we had offices in the Gwinnett Federal Building, we were coming down in an elevator and I told him we were going to a closing, and he asked, 'Are we buying or selling?'" But in the late 1980s, Jimmy was ready to step back and asked Wayne to buy him out in cash. Tom Martin, who was a banker in Duluth, explained, "Jimmy told me one time that he was richer than all the rest of his friends, richer than his brother Wayne, or John D. Stephens, or Virgil Williams. Not understanding what he was thinking, and knowing the other people involved, I asked him, 'How is that?' Jimmy came back saying, 'I've got more than they have, for I have [all I need].'"[29]

Ten years later, Jimmy was on a trade mission to São Paulo, Brazil, on behalf of the Georgia Ports Authority when he had the accident that would cause his death. While walking around the city on May 9, 1998, he tripped over a utility pole wire that sent him tumbling face-first onto the sidewalk. Tom Dillon, who was on the trip, remembered, "Jimmy was walking just in front of me, a couple of feet. He was walking ahead of us but looking backwards, talking to us. Had I not been walking behind and looking forward, I might have hit the wire, too."[30] The delegation took Jimmy to the hotel, then a clinic, but he seemed to be feeling better. That next Monday, he remained in the hotel while the others attended a meeting and spoke to his wife, Doris, and his daughter Tina for a few minutes. Later that afternoon, he came down for dinner but did not eat and returned to his room. Dillon went to check on him and recalled, "When he came to the door, he wasn't feeling well, and went to sit on the bed. Jimmy did not realize he had a serious head injury, and coupled with him taking a blood thinner, we later learn that blood was escaping into his head cavity. When we sat down on the bed, he told me that he thought he was dying."[31]

Realizing the seriousness of the situation, they took him to the hospital, and Jimmy's family flew to Brazil. They decided to bring him home in an air ambulance, but despite his excellent care, he died on June 5, 1998. Richard Tucker remembered the impact on his brother. "Wayne was not one to show a lot of emotion, but I knew him well enough. It was a deep blow. Jimmy was three years older, and Wayne had never lived without Jimmy. They had two sisters, but the brothers were a tight team, so his death had an impact, even if invisible to others."[32] Bartow Morgan, a longtime business associate, echoed the point: "Wayne is a problem solver. When something bad or tragic happened, he focused on the outcome: 'How do I solve this? How do

I help his family? How do I keep the businesses going?' Not many people got to see his emotional side."[33] Wayne summed up the loss: "We were together every day from the time I can remember. We were a great team, and I miss him even today."[34]

The Mason Family, 1926.

*Courtesy Tracey Mason*

J. P. Mason and Emma Williams Mason, Wayne's grandparents.

*Courtesy Tracey Mason*

Wayne Mason, 1949.

*Courtesy Tracey Mason*

High school sweethearts, Ann Biggers and Wayne Mason, 1957.

*Courtesy Ann and Wayne Mason*

Wayne Mason in his senior year of high school, 1958.

*Courtesy Ann and Wayne Mason*

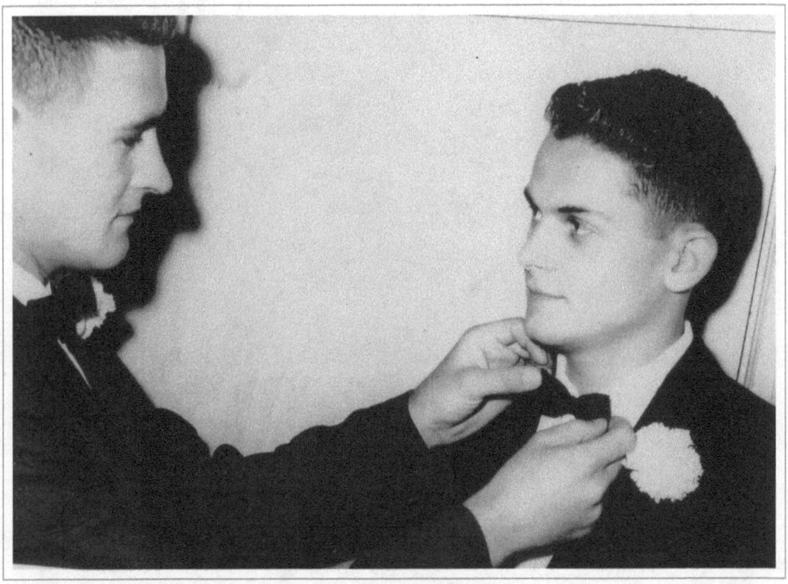

Jimmy and Wayne Mason,
at Wayne and Ann Mason's wedding, 1959.

*Courtesy Tracey Mason*

Cousins Keith and Tracey Mason, 1964.

*Courtesy Tracey Mason*

Wayne Mason outside Snellville Baptist Church, 1968.

*Courtesy Ann and Wayne Mason*

Wayne and Ann Mason with their four children, 1971.

*Courtesy Ann and Wayne Mason*

Wayne, Jimmy, and their father, J. Winston Mason, 1973.

*Courtesy Ann and Wayne Mason*

Stanley Gunter, a friend and owner of a barbeque restaurant on U.S. 29 in Lawrenceville, modified Wayne Mason's campaign poster and put it up in his restaurant.

*Courtesy Ann and Wayne Mason*

Commissioner Wayne Mason, 1976.
Courtesy Ann and Wayne Mason

Wayne Mason at the Lake Lanier
water intake groundbreaking, 1977.

Re-election Poster for Wayne Mason,
Gwinnett Commission, 1980.

*Courtesy Ann and Wayne Mason*

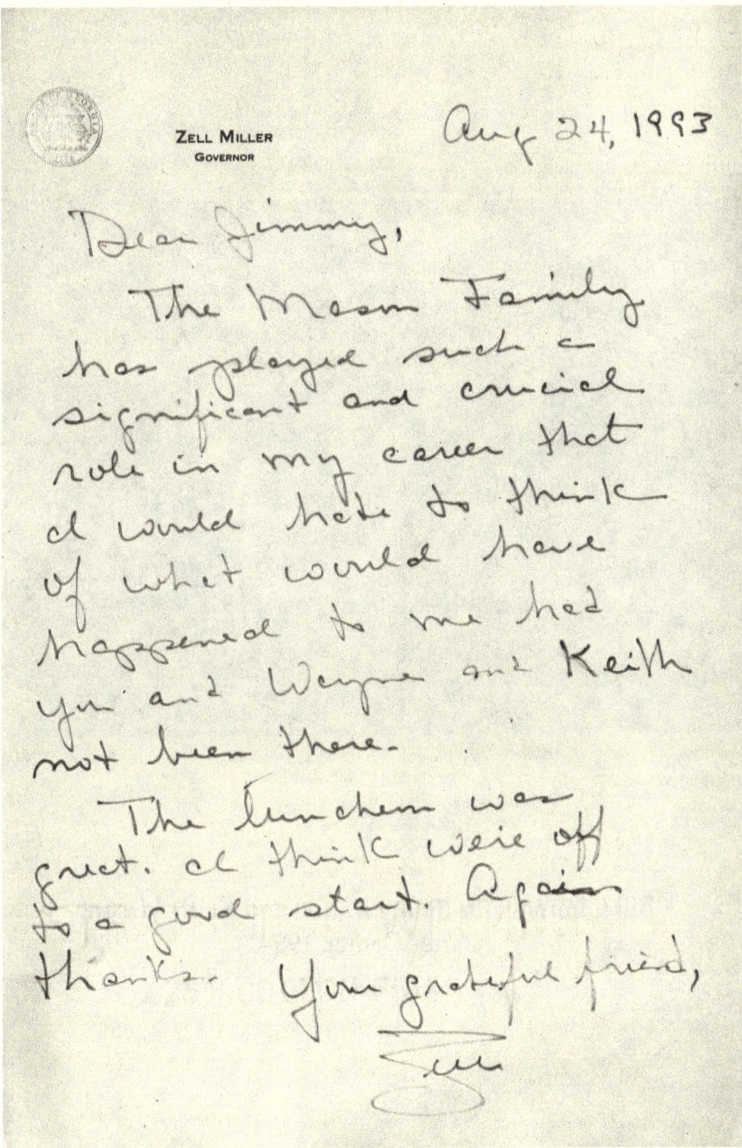

Zell Miller
Governor

Aug 24, 1993

Dear Jimmy,

The Mason Family has played such a significant and crucial role in my career that I would hate to think of what would have happened to me had you and Wayne and Keith not been there.

The luncheon was great. I think we're off to a good start. Again thanks.

Your grateful friend,

Zell

Zell Miller letter to Jimmy Mason, 1993.

*Courtesy Tracey Mason*

Bill Clinton with Jimmy Mason and Keith Mason,
Carter Center, 1994.

*Courtesy Tracey Mason*

The Mason family, 1994.

*Courtesy Ann and Wayne Mason*

Wayne Mason (center) photographed with Richard Tucker and David Seago, receiving the Gwinnett Chamber of Commerce, Citizen of the Year Award, 1999.

*Courtesy Ann and Wayne Mason*

Wayne Mason with a map of the property he purchased along the Beltline, 2005.

*Courtesy Ann and Wayne Mason*

The Mason Family, 2009.

*Courtesy Ann and Wayne Mason*

The Mason Family, 2015.

*Courtesy Ann and Wayne Mason*

Wayne Mason in his office, 2022.

*Courtesy Gwinnett Magazine*

# Chapter 6

## A New Era: From Braselton to the Beltline

> "If they keep on building, there ain't going to be nothing left to build on." —B. M. Jackson, 1985

The 1980s transformed Gwinnett County, setting the trajectory for its future. While it had been growing since World War II, the 1980s represented a crossroads. As Bill Kirby writes, "To some the growth was a wonderful thing—more jobs, international business ties, fancier cars, bigger homes, better schools. But to others, it was endless traffic, crowded classrooms, overflowing sewers and unbridled commercialism."[1] B. M. Jackson, a longtime Norcross resident who retired after a career in carpentry, expressed his displeasure in 1985: "It's not benefiting me in any way, but there's lots of people that it is. If they keep on building, there ain't going to be nothing left to build on."[2] Another resident, Jona Cheek, had a more moderated response: "The traffic's real bad, but everyone's still on speaking terms. All this growth's brought businesses to town. I think it's great myself."[3]

After Jimmy Mason's retirement in 1988 and subsequent death a decade later, Wayne extended his business activities from a focus mainly in Gwinnett County to other parts of metropolitan Atlanta and half a dozen other Southeastern states. He established dozens of limited partnerships for each project and attracted other investors to his business projects. But he would gain publicity from two projects in particular: buying land in Braselton from Kim Basinger and purchasing the land from Norfolk Southern that would become part of the Atlanta Beltline, a pedestrian-oriented ring developed around the city's railroad corridor that included mixed-use retail, housing, parks, and trails. Wayne had a particular philosophy about real estate: "You got to be patient, and you never get mad. People may treat you mean, but you have to keep your cool, for in the long run, you can get even."[4] This approach has helped shape the county for the last forty years.

## Buying Braselton

In 1989, Georgia-born actress Kim Basinger, in partnership with the pension fund of the Chicago telecommunications giant Ameritech Corporation, purchased 1,800 acres of land in Braselton, Georgia, for $20 million with the goal of establishing movie and recording studios. Writing for the *Chicago Tribune*, Bill Osinski explains, "The glamorous but hazy plan was to transform Braselton into a tourist attraction with major recording and movie production studios."[5] But as her brother Mick Basinger explained in 1992, "With the current state of the economy, it's difficult to find investment partners you want to get in bed with." A poorly timed recession ultimately killed the project, and Wayne Mason and Frank Hanna (Wayne's oldest daughter Kim Hanna's father-in-law) purchased 1,740 acres of this land in Braselton for $4.5 million in 1995, making it one of his most important deals during this period.

Wayne recalled that the Ameritech Pension Fund sent a representative to Gwinnett:

> I think they told him just get rid of the land at any price. This young executive was in Atlanta at a lawyer's office, and they got me on the phone. I had made an offer to them of $4 million for the property, and he said he would not take one penny less than $5 million. I told him I would split the difference with him, but once we hung up the phone, my offer was off the table. I also asked him if he had looked out the window of an airplane when he came down here, he would have seen that the land had been vacant since the Braseltons bought it in 1840. I asked, since it hadn't been developed from that time, what was I going to do with it?[6]

The land was spread between four counties: Gwinnett, Jackson, Barrow, and Hall. As Wayne explained, "It was the right place at the right time. Atlanta was growing north, and this purchase was following the growth."[7]

They agreed on the $4.5 million deal, and Wayne agreed to forego the environmental study. He explained, "They were worried that the study might come back saying the land was contaminated, so they knocked off half what the environmental study would have cost, $300,000, or $150,000 off, and we bought it for $4.35 million."[8] After the sale, Wayne said,

> we got all the land, plus some houses, almost everything in Braselton, for $2,800 an acre in 1995. When I had the first sale to the Weeks Corporation, I made back my purchase price, for I sold them 100 acres for $4.6 million in 2000. It was several years before we made the first sale, but the Braselton property was

> probably the finest deal we've ever made. In 2005, ten years after we bought the Braselton property, we sold more than 300 acres to Duke Realty Corporation for a little over $20 million.[9]

## King of the Deal

The Braselton project was just one of many of Wayne Mason's deals that helped develop the county. As the *Atlanta Constitution* reported in 2005, "Mason bought and sold the land for Discover Mills mall in Duluth. He pressed for the construction of Ronald Regan Parkway, which transformed farmland he owned outside Snellville into prime property for everything from a Target to a multiplex cinema. He has brokered deals for Walmart stores and been the spark behind countless subdivisions."[10] Not everyone supported the explosive growth, as the *Atlanta Constitution* reported: "They are the kind of developments that turn soccer moms into sign-waiving activists and breed hatred among tree-loving environmentalists. These folks see Mason as a developer who builds without regard for the consequences: traffic congestion and overcrowded schools."[11]

In this era, Wayne was working out of his office at 1505 Lakes Parkway in Lawrenceville, sharing a building with Andersen, Tate, Mahaffey & McGarity; Gwinnett Partners; Madison Ventures; and Arlington Capital—all companies that he had ties to as a client, mentor, investor, or partner. One journalist explained that to understand Wayne's approach to business, you just needed to look at his two cell phones. Wayne explained, "When someone has something to sell, they're going to sell it to the first person they talk to. If they can't find you, they'll sell it to someone else. If you're not accessible, you're not successful."[12]

Mason's development model—called "birthing and burying"—might have seemed somewhat unconventional. He assembled partners for a project, created a corporation for each one, and dissolved the corporation when the land was sold. Putting the team together was key.

> Mason typically puts up the money to buy tracts that partners can't afford. In return, the partners manage the details of the transaction—such as rezonings and site work—with oversight from Mason and his attorneys. That frees up Mason to troll for the next hot deal. With most projects, he claims 50 percent of the profits and a 12 percent return on investment. The remaining is divided up among the partners. He explains, "I put up all the money, put up all the risk. They do all the work, and we split the profit. That is the way I operate."[13]

In each case, Mason and his partners would buy large tracts of land, resell it to commercial or residential builders, often in smaller parcels, and pocket the profits. By 2005, he was working in seven Southeastern states. While he was a builder early in his career, that shifted in the 1980s and 1990s. But eventually he realized there was a better way. "Mason says he doesn't build anything now. He leaves that to his partners. Instead, his goal is to find undervalued land that he can buy and recast for another more valuable use. In the business, developers call it 'highest and best use.'"[14] This is possible because of his depth and breadth of experience. "My real expertise is knowing value. I can look at some property and tell you right away what it's worth. It takes a lifetime to learn how to do that."[15] When criticized for his approach,

> Mason also said his opponents fail to recognize that Gwinnett's aggressive development deserves credit for its top-notch school system, robust economy, and a strong job base that employs 60 percent of the county's working residents. That's why the value of shopping centers, office parks, subdivisions, and roads is far greater than the wealth they've brought him. He explains, "Everything begins and ends with the jobs. If you're not growing, you're dying."[16]

Five major projects illustrate Wayne's approach. In the 1980s, Wayne, his son Keith, and several other partners bought 224 acres at the intersection of what would become Ronald Regan Parkway and GA 124, which would become Presidential Market Center. In a decade, Mason turned the property into a shopping center and made $22.6 million. He later developed other commercial centers, thus creating a connected commercial corridor that has helped drive growth. Wayne also worked with Mills Corporation to develop Discover Mills on a 22.5-acre site. The 1.3 million-square-foot outlet center became an anchor commercial property in Gwinnett, as did the Crossroads at Gwinnett, a 195-acre site that included retail, industrial, apartment, and office space. Anchored by a Walmart, Mason sold the property for more than $34 million, more than twice what he paid for it. He did a similar deal with the Chapel Station subdivision in Lawrenceville. There, he turned an $830,000 investment into a $2.2 million project that was sold as fifty-five individual lots. The Villages at Global Forum became one of the county's first live-work-play developments. The seventy acres near Buford Highway and I-285 brought hundreds of apartments and 100,000 square feet of commercial space. Each of these deals shows the power of Wayne's model and helped Gwinnett become a powerhouse among metropolitan Atlanta counties.

But Wayne's reach went beyond Atlanta, extending throughout the state and region. One of his most significant development opportunities involved the Port of Savannah. The port dates from 1733, when General James Edward Oglethorpe arrived on Yamacraw Bluff on the Savannah River to create the new colony of Georgia and city of Savannah. Cash crops soon became profitable, which helped Savannah develop into one of the leading cotton-shipping ports in the world. It is located on the border between Georgia and South Carolina, eighteen miles inland from the Atlantic Ocean at the mouth of the Savannah River. The port played a critical role in the Civil War and World War II. Recognizing the port's significance and potential for growth, the Georgia Ports Authority (GPA) was established by the Georgia General Assembly on March 9, 1945. The agency was charged "to do any other things necessary to foster or encourage the commerce, domestic or foreign, of the state, the United States of America, or the several sister states."[17] Three years later, the GPA bought land in nearby Garden City to open the Garden City Terminal (completed in 1950). In 1958, the port opened a second ocean terminal from land they purchased from the Central of Georgia Railway. In 1962, the ocean terminal was renovated and three new berths were added to Garden City. The first containerized cargo ship arrived in Savannah Harbor in 1965, and four years later, Container Berth 1 was added to the

Garden City Terminal. By 1972, ships from Japan were arriving in Savannah, and the port was undergoing constant transformation, including the 1985 purchase of 2,200 acres from Drakies Plantation and the 1992 widening of the port by five hundred feet.[18] Summing up the growth in this era, Mary Ann DeMuth explained in *Georgia Trend*, that "over the years, GPA acquired more land, steadily made improvements and recognized the tremendous efficiency gains that could be achieved through the ability to handle cargo shipped in large containers. By the 1970s, the first container terminal had opened in Savannah and a second one was on the drawing board."[19]

Wayne Mason and his partners had an opportunity to buy about 1,200 acres in Savannah in the mid-2000s as the port was undergoing extensive growth. Keith Mason, now a partner at Long, Aldridge & Norman, was appointed by Zell Miller to the Georgia Port Authority in 1998 and served as a board member from 1998 to 2005 and as chair from 2001 to 2003. He recalled, "When I joined the board, we barely had enough operating funds for three months. We were paying too much in debt, which prevented any realistic growth. One of my jobs was to help rework the financial package to put us on firmer footing."[20]

Trained as a lawyer, Keith began studying the port, making regular trips to Savannah and reading trade publications to get a sense of how the area might be developed. As Keith was completing his service on the GPA, both he and Wayne realized that the port lacked available Class A distribution warehouses. Class A warehouses are state-of-the-art properties designed and built specifically to benefit the supply chain and can transform how a port operates; they were essential additions to the Port of Savannah. Today, the port is the number one export container port and third largest in the nation, the number one export container and third largest gateway in the nation.

## Building the Beltline

One of Wayne's most significant recent projects is the Atlanta Beltline. Atlanta has always been a railroad town, having been built as the terminal point of the Western & Atlantic Railroad in the 1830s. Traffic and congestion have long been a struggle for the region, and it is consistently ranked one of the top ten for commute times in the nation, a dubious distinction. Regional leaders have long sought solutions and proposed projects to develop alternative development opportunities. In 1999, a novel idea was put forth from an unlikely source. Georgia Tech student Ryan Gravel wrote a master's thesis entitled "Belt Line—Atlanta: Design and Infrastructure as a Reflection of Public Policy" and proposed reclaiming the city's railroad corridor and "transforming it into a new public transit system combined with economic development and connectivity strategies."[21] A native of Atlanta, Gravel was inspired by his time in Paris without a car. He hated driving on the I-285 corridor and decided to dedicate his studies to coming up with a creative solution. As the *Atlanta Journal-Constitution* reported, "His story is now Atlanta folklore, how a young, aspirational fellow with a simple yet outlandish idea could engender such change.... Gravel turned in his thesis, which proposed that a loop of 22 miles of mostly abandoned rail lines be repurposed as transit lines connecting neighborhoods."[22]

Gravel's idea was not novel; others had proposed a similar plan as early as the 1960s, as detailed in Mark Pendergrast's book *City on the Verge*. Sam Williams, the former chief executive officer of the Metropolitan Chamber of Commerce, remembered "taking a train tour in the fall of 1972 with Franklin Garrett, the longtime historian at the Atlanta History Center. We toured the Beltline, looking at warehouses, Civil War sites, and talked about the potential development in the area. Plenty of people saw the economic opportunities because there was so much there, all abandoned and available dirt cheap."[23] There was also a study done in 1989 by the Rails to Trails Conservancy and a second study done in 1990 called the "Cultural Ring" by PATH Foundation, a nonprofit founded in 1991 to turn "abandoned railroad corridors into beautiful linear green spaces [that] linked neighborhoods to bustling commercial centers and provided alternative modes of transportation for commuters, joggers, walkers, cyclists and people of all ages."[24]

But Gravel's passion got all the attention and helped seal the deal. As Bill Torpy reports, "In 2001, he put together a packet with his plan and some maps and sent them to all the powers and politicos he could think of—the governor, the mayor, MARTA, the Georgia Department of Transportation...and Cathy Woolard, then head of the City Council's transportation committee."[25] Woolard responded enthusiastically and asked him to join a public meeting, which turned into a series of meetings with city council members, neighbors, developers, and those advocating for trails, parks, and affordable housing. By 2003, the project's promotion was underway.

In 2004, Wayne and Keith bought seventy-two acres from Norfolk Southern for $25 million. Wayne was on a train to Chicago and heard about the land from Cathy

Woolard. Not long after, a real estate broker, J. William Butler, representing Norfolk Southern came to his office to make a deal. As Wayne remembered it, "He said I can deliver the land from I-85 to Dekalb Avenue. I want $250,000 in earnest money, and I can close in 90 days. I went over to Brand Bank to get the check and then hired an engineering firm to survey the whole tract, run the title, and work with the EPA to do a brownfield review. It went really fast, and a lot of Atlanta developers were stunned."[26]

The land stretched from Ansley Park to the Old Fourth Ward, one of the most coveted pieces of the Beltline project that comprised 20 percent of the loop. Along with his son Keith, Wayne now owned five miles of the twenty-two-mile Beltline path. The project became quite controversial, leading the Masons to issue a statement after they decided to sell the land just three years later.

> More than 2 ½ years ago, we invested in the City's vision for a public-private partnership and committed to do our part to realize the Beltline concept and potential. We offered to donate to the City 43 acres of property for 11 parks and 5 ½ miles of double-tracked transit and rail. Throughout the 5 ½ mile corridor, we proposed creating 3,000 housing units and 140,000 square feet of retail. The plan was unacceptable to the City's initial top Beltline advisors as well as some City officials, who, working in concert with special interest opponents, made the process untenable. We analyzed our options and are pleased with the sale of our Beltline property interests. It was a valuable investment for us and we believe it will be even more valuable for future owners. We regret that our proposals were not accepted by the City's previ-

> ous Beltline leaders. We believe with the new Beltline leadership headed by Terri Montague that the new owners and the City will have a rewarding relationship.[27]

In 2007, Keith Mason negotiated the sale of the Mason's sixty-six acres to new owners, headed by developer Ben Raney of Barry Real Estate, for $66 million. But that's where things got complicated.

Barry Real Estate formed a partnership with the city's nonprofit Atlanta Beltline Inc. (ABI). The goal was for ABI to purchase the land for $66 million and maintain control. Barry contributed $1.5 million and was going to help raise the funds and work as a consultant. The original plan was to pay the Masons $25 million and then $450,000 monthly until they settled the debt on October 31, 2008. Buckhead attorney John Woodham sued the city for using school taxes to fund the Beltline and won. Eventually, the Georgia Supreme Court ruled that tax allocation districts could not use educational funds for such projects.[28] The resulting negotiations between Barry and ABI became even more contentious, and Woodham questioned the legality of the entire enterprise: "What strikes me from my initial review of the documentation is that the entire deal may have been facially illegal under state law from the outset. It appears this joint venture deal between a public body and a private company could have been a violation of the Georgia Local Government Public Works Construction Law."[29] This all unfolded in the midst of a major recession that started in 2006 with declining housing prices. By October 2008, Congress approved a $700 billion bank bailout, and in February 2009, President Barack Obama put forth a $787 economic stimulus package to stave off a depression that had global implications.[30]

The failure of the Masons and the City of Atlanta to come to an agreement in 2005 and 2006 had a complicated history. Hattie Dorsey, a longtime affordable housing advocate and consultant for the Masons on the Beltline, offered one explanation:

> When Wayne Mason bought the land, nobody was really paying attention to how important it was. But when a developer from Gwinnett County became involved, the city took notice. At the time, Gwinnett County was seen as a racist county, and because Wayne lived there, he was tarred with the same brush. The City of Atlanta and other business leaders asked: "What is this white man doing buying up all this land?" It had been in their backyard all this time, but they never showed any interest or vision. They were especially mad that they had no way to control him. It was all politics. But Wayne had a good idea to create mixed-income housing that was blended with retail. They did not trust him or treat him fairly, and the city lost a lot of money and time because of that short-sightedness.[31]

Sam Williams, former chief operating officer of the Metropolitan Atlanta Chamber of Commerce, recalled, "Wayne was pushing uphill to create affordable housing, but the city did not want an OTP [outside the perimeter] developer from Gwinnett to get the credit."[32] Even with the complications of this reality, Wayne was still proud of his work with the Beltline, keeping a front-page story about it from the *Atlanta Business Chronicle* framed on his office wall. When asked about it, in typical fashion, he reflected on the ups and downs of his career. But he never waivers in his belief that he really never loses anything, because "I never had anything to start with."[33]

## Made a Lot, Lost a Lot

While Wayne Mason was able to extricate himself from the Beltline controversy, the recession played havoc on his businesses. As Dan Chapman reports in the *Atlanta Journal-Constitution*, "Homes, shopping centers, warehouses, up-scale communities—all Mason ventures at one time or an-other—have lost immense value and left their developers in deep financial trouble."[34] Wayne reflected on the challenges at the time and explained, "I've made a lot of money and lost a lot of money, more in this recession than in any oth-er." He went on to explain that "every sector of the real estate industry has taken a hit."[35] And Wayne was not spared.

In October 2009, Wachovia Bank sued him for default-ing on a $75 million loan in relation to several units in a Buckhead medical building. A month later, he was sued with several partners for $42.5 million in loans to finance Hampton Island Preserve on the Georgia coast. In 2015, the Mason family was sued in US District Court for $137 mil-lion for allegedly fraudulently transferring assets to keep them from creditors. The suit claimed three things. First, Wayne was accused of declaring his net worth as $169.8 million in 2007, but not disclosing $248.7 million in liabili-ties from real estate assets. Second, he stopped paying credi-tors and told lenders in March 2010 that his net worth was negative $223.7 million. Finally, Wayne was accused of making "over $100 million in real estate transfers" to relatives, other companies, and a family trust, including cash, stocks, and land along the Atlanta Beltline just as the economy was moving toward recession in 2007.[36] The suit alleged that "Wayne made the Transfers with actual intent to hinder, delay, or defraud his present and future creditors, such as Plaintiff." The 2015 suit grew out of two civil judgments in Liberty and Gwinnett Counties that argued that, as result of defaulted real estate loans, Wayne owed $6 million. As reported by the *Atlanta Constitution*, "The rights to those judgments later were sold to a third party, Edgefield Holdings, which is suing to collect the debts." Mason was represented by former governor Roy Barnes, who declared, "We do not believe that the case has any foundation or is meritorious. We look forward to a favorable resolution on the matter on our behalf."[37] There were multiple lawsuits during this time, and because Wayne was the main guarantor of the loans, the banks focused mainly on him. It took several years to untangle all of the complex issues, but settlements were made in 2016 resolving all the outstanding issues.

In a long career, taking big risks and accepting losses is part of the game. Elliott Brack, who wrote a history of Gwinnett County, reflects on Wayne's resilience: "You're going to lose a few and be sued and give up some property—most people don't pitch no-hitters every day. But he'll come back strong. When it comes to investing, he's as good as they come."[38]

# Chapter 7

## Giving Back and Passing the Torch

> "Gwinnett has been a great place, it's been good to me. What I want to be known for is as a giver, not a taker. Some want to take, take, take. To me, it's about giving."—Wayne Mason

The rural county in which Wayne and Jimmy Mason grew up has changed in ways that would have been hard for them to imagine when they began their real estate business. As Elliott Brack argues, "With the rapid growth of commercial activity in Gwinnett, and with the continuing influx of new residents occupying burgeoning homebuilding industry output, for a while there seemed little attention given to cultural needs—the theater, fine arts, and other activities."[1] Starting in the 1980s, that began to change, and the community's recreational, medical, educational, cultural, and athletic resources and activities began to flourish. A 2023 report published by the Atlanta Regional Commission documents how much has changed in the past forty years, reporting that Gwinnett is now home to 1,224 businesses related to creative industries that employ 13,723 people and has 241 cultural nonprofits that bring in $117,171,193 in revenue to the county.[2] But community building cannot take place without a broad and sustained commitment to philanthropy.

That commitment came from people like Paula Bagwell, a member of the Lawrenceville Women's Club who worked to establish an arts council that was formalized as the Gwinnett Council for the Arts in 1981. The council moved first to the old Lawrenceville Post Office and eventually worked to raise money to build a Fine Arts Center. This was about the time that the county began discussions about building a civic center and cultural center (now the Gas South District) that would include a space for performing and visual arts. Nancy Gullickson, who took over the arts council, worked to raise funds for the arts component of the project. Developer Scott Hudgens agreed to give an anonymous million-dollar gift in 1991 and a $2 million gift nearly a decade later to support the children's museum. Another developer, Ray Weeks, gave $150,000 for an outdoor sculpture garden in memory of his father, and Frank Rowe and his family gave funds to name the promenade at the children's museum. Additional gifts from the Lettie Pate Evans Foundation, the Frances Wood Wilson Foundation, and the Robert W. Woodruff Foundation helped grow the center. The fine arts complex, named the Jaqueline Casey Hudgens Center for Art and Learning, was named the "best suburban arts venue" in 1997.[3] Other cultural institutions include the Gwinnett History Museum, the Gwinnett Philharmonic, the Aurora Theater, and half a dozen other community theaters.

Gwinnett's record in community-building is impressive. Organizations such as Scientific-Atlanta, based in Lawrenceville, had long committed resources to encourage students to engage in STEM and engineering careers. Even though the company was acquired by Cisco Systems in California for $6.9 billion in 2005, their commitment to Gwinnett has endured. John Riddle, Scientific America's vice president of marketing and development, argues, "It often takes a company like theirs to step up and be the first to say OK, here's what we are going to do to help."[4] They are just one of the many companies and individuals who have made commitments to philanthropy. More recently, Clyde and Sandra Strickland have been recognized for their giving to the library system in the county, notably a $1 million donation to the public library in Lawrenceville.[5] In 2016, the Stricklands also gave $1 million to the Gwinnett Medical Center to fund the development of a family medical center.

The Masons have a long history of philanthropy in the county, often reflecting Wayne's philosophy: "I try to help people when I can, especially those who I know obviously need it. You are known for what you give away, not for what you try to take with you."[6] His family's work with the Atlanta Food Bank, the Boy Scouts, hospitals, youth sports, and local churches and parks reflect the broad, but often unnoticed, impact on the county and region. Wayne often says, "I have given away lots of money, which people do not know about, and I want to keep it that way."[7] Despite a long history of giving, Keith Mason explains that his father's generosity often slips under the radar and is often anonymous—from donating land for churches to helping establish parks and ballfields and raising education funds throughout the county.[8] Wayne's niece Tracey Mason explains, "It's a family tradition to serve the community. I was always told—and shown—that you have to give something back. You have to leave the world a better place. Uncle Wayne has always been dogged in his pursuit to make a deal, but he is generous almost to a fault."[9]

One area of Wayne's engagement is helping to foster the next generation of leaders. In the 1980s, eleven business leaders led by Jack Sawyer decided to create Leadership Gwinnett, a year-long program that would focus on issues facing the county with the goal of coming up with creative solutions. As one participant explained, "This is not a program to prepare you to run for office, but to prepare you for leadership wherever you go. By your selection for this program, you are a leader already. This program will make you a better one." Wayne was an active participant, as Peter Boyce (of the inaugural group) recalled: "The icons of Gwinnett opened our eyes to what made Gwinnett so great. To have the opportunity to get face to face with the colorful Wayne Mason, the detail-oriented Wayne Shackelford, to have Governor Zell Miller come to our fall retreat and to get the benefit of a world of knowledge from local historians boosted most of our lives both professionally and personally."[10]

Wayne's community engagement also involves direct philanthropy. In 1984, a group of community leaders, driven by Superintendent Alton Crews, formed Gwinnett Foundation Inc. (now the Community Foundation of Northeast Georgia) and named Charles R. Brown as the first president. The foundation's goal was "to be the one place within Gwinnett that people could go to find out key needs of the community and raise money to meet such needs."[11] Early projects included buying land for Parkview High School to create community soccer fields. In 1987, Robert Fowler, who recently sold the *Gwinnett Daily News*, offered a $1 million challenge grant for the community to match to support the YMCA. Wayne recalled a meeting to discuss how to make that happen: "There are about 20 of us here in the room, so that makes $50,000 each of us has to either raise or pay. And we went out there and raised the money."[12]

The Atlanta Community Food Bank is an especially important charity for the Mason family. Wayne explained, "No one should go hungry in this country. If I can help stop that, I will." The food bank has a long history in the city of Atlanta. Bill Bolling had worked as director of the community kitchen at St. Luke's Episcopal Church in downtown Atlanta before founding the food bank in 1979. That first year, they partnered with twenty-five community groups and distributed more than 15,000 pounds of food. Four years after its founding, the food bank moved from the basement of St. Luke's to a warehouse on Whitehall Street. Soon to outgrow that space, the food bank moved to 970 Jefferson Street and worked out of the former Anheuser-Busch warehouse for the next twenty years. To promote awareness about hunger, the food bank has hosted a Hunger Walk, Atlanta's Table (a program where food is picked up from restaurants, hotels, and caterers and delivered to agencies that can help distribute it quickly), community gardens, and the "Kids in Need" program.[13] In 2004, the food bank moved to 732 Joseph E. Lowry Boulevard. With a small group of business leaders, Wayne helped raise $125,000 for the new building. His support of the food bank reflects his perspective on giving: "I tell everybody, 'Listen, after you eat all you need to eat, and your family eats all they need to eat, then, hell, let somebody else eat. Don't be so damn greedy.'"[14]

Wayne also worked to help move the former railroad depot to Mountain Park. Mike Barnett, head of the Mountain Park Jaycees, had worked for years to develop a community center. He recalled reading about Mary Beth Busbee, Governor George Busbee's wife, who was preserving railroad depots in the state.

> You see, the railroad was taking down abandoned depots because of the liability insurance. When approaching Mary Beth with the idea of a depot for our community center, she loved the idea, and started searching for the person I should approach. She was very helpful, and eventually suggested I talk to the Interstate Commerce Commission in Washington. It just so happened that this was the year I was taking our young daughters to Washington. While there after talking to bureaucrats all day, I finally found an ICC official I needed to talk to, of course with Mary Beth's help. He gave me a letter with his blessings to the Southern Railway officials in Atlanta.[15]

They eventually found a depot in Shannon, Georgia, and had it moved for $7,000. But converting the depot to a community center was not cheap, and Wayne Mason, K.C. Bowen, and Wayne Shackleford worked for several years to help the depot become the centerpiece of the community.

Wayne's giving also supported the growth of churches in the county. In partnership with Virgil Williams, Wayne gave away a multimillion dollar parcel that he had purchased from Boeing near Interstate I-85 to Cross Point Church. The church was started by Reverend James Merritt, who had been Wayne's pastor at the First Baptist Church in Snellville in 2003. He explained, "We gave them 74 acres of land, plus 280,000 square feet of building space, including 100,000 square feet for offices. The church gets 2,000 people attending services each Sunday."[16] Wayne and Virgil spread the gift over a three-year period, making it possible for the new church to grow and thrive.

When the Gwinnett County Chamber of Commerce needed a new space in 1998, having outgrown a building near Gwinnett Tech, Wayne and his friends sprang into action. Richard Tucker recalled that they needed a space that would allow for growth and hired John O'Kane of Cox-Curry Associates to help raise funds. Major donors included Scott Hudgens, who had the board of directors room named for longtime chamber president Jack Sawyer and former legislator Jimmy Mason; Wayne Mason, for whom the atrium was named; and John Stephens, for whom the education room named.[17] The team eventually raised $3.2 million, and with long-term financing, the total $6.5 million project was funded.

Longtime associate Bartow Morgan recalled that

> when I was looking to spend time or money to support our community, I often went to Wayne for advice. He had a really good sense of what was needed and where the dollars should be focused. One area that he really had an impact on was Georgia Gwinnett College. He was in the forefront of working to get that put together. He contributed his energy and connections to start the college and gave a leadership grant to help set expectations for other business leaders to become involved. Wayne was one of the original trustees. He believed that a county of our size—which was fast approaching a million people—really needed a good college that had a strong nursing pro-

> gram. He knew it would serve our students and raise the profile of Gwinnett. In order to attract new residents, you have to have good schools, housing, and hospitals, and the business community can help build all of that.[18]

Georgia Gwinnett College opened in 2006 with 118 students, and the first thirty-eight students graduated in 2008. Wayne has served on its board since the school first opened and is especially proud of its growth. Today, "*U.S. News & World Report* has ranked GGC the most ethnically diverse Southern regional college for its ninth consecutive year (2015–2023) and the #12 top public Southern regional college for 2023."[19]

There are a dozen additional organizations that Wayne has supported, helping libraries, children, and area medical facilities. He has also been a longtime supporter of the Boy Scouts of America, and Wayne and his partners donated 200 acres for the Black Creek Scout Reservation, between Savannah and Sea Island, which remains an active site for the organization. Wayne has donated resources and served on the Gwinnett Medical Center Foundation Board. He and Bartow Morgan Jr. helped raise $15 million for a new heart center. There are few nonprofits in Gwinnett County that Wayne or the Mason family have not helped support over the years.

## Honors Abound

Wayne Mason's energy is boundless, but he rarely talks about his successes, and even less about any recognition he has received. On May 6, 2019, the Georgia General Assembly designed the Wayne Mason Highway through House

Resolution 346, Part XV. The formal language of the resolution reveals the depth and breadth of Wayne's impact. It holds:

> WHEREAS, Mr. Wayne Mason has long been recognized by the citizens of this state for the vital role that he has played in leadership and his deep personal commitment to the welfare of the citizens of Georgia; and
>
> WHEREAS, a native of Gwinnett County, Mr. Mason is the founder and president of Mason Family Companies, which invests and develops single-family and multifamily properties and commercial and industrial developments throughout metropolitan Atlanta and the Southeast; and
>
> WHEREAS, just a few of Mr. Mason's accomplishments with Mason Family Companies include developing the 300 acre Cisco Systems corporate campus; Gwinnett County's first mixed use project, Global Forum; Duluth's first mixed use project, Crossroads; 400 Commons in Forsyth County; assembling property for Discover Mills in Lawrenceville; and planning of redevelopment which helped spur the City of Atlanta's Beltline; and
>
> WHEREAS, Mr. Mason served on the Gwinnett County Board of Commissioners from 1972 to 1980, where his tenure was marked with numerous accomplishments, including developing lasting relationships with bond and finance houses which led to county infrastructure improvements such as a new water treatment plant, more than 800 miles of roads, a county-wide fire protection network, Gwinnett's first modern police headquarters, the county's first

land use plan, and the county's first business licensing program; and

WHEREAS, he has diligently and conscientiously devoted innumerable hours of his time, talents, and energy toward the betterment of his community and state as evidenced dramatically by his superlative service on behalf of Gwinnett County, serving as a board member of the Gwinnett County Chamber of Commerce, Council for Quality Growth, Georgia Gwinnett College Foundation, and Gwinnett Medical Center Foundation; and

WHEREAS, Mr. Mason has been recognized with numerous honors and accolades, including Citizen of the Year Award from the Gwinnett County Chamber of Commerce and a Button Gwinnett Award for lifetime public and professional contributions from the Council for Quality Growth; and

WHEREAS, it is abundantly fitting and proper that this remarkable and distinguished Georgian be recognized appropriately by dedicating a road in his honor.

THEREFORE, BE IT RESOLVED AND ENACTED BY THE GENERAL ASSEMBLY OF GEORGIA, that the portion of US-78 in Gwinnett County, from the city of Snellville, to the city of Loganville, is dedicated as the Wayne Mason Highway.

BE IT FURTHER RESOLVED, that the Department of Transportation is authorized and directed to erect and maintain appropriate signs dedicating the road facilities named in this Resolution.

BE IT FURTHER RESOLVED, that the Clerk of the House of Representatives is authorized and di-

> rected to make appropriate copies of this Resolution available for distribution to the Department of Transportation and the family of Mr. Wayne Mason.[20]

A year later, in December 2020, Wayne was honored with a sculpture and plaque at the Shoal Creek Water Filter Plant to honor his involvement in the development of Gwinnett's water system. What might seem like an unusual honor confirms Wayne's belief that Gwinnett's future was always going to be tied to water. If you controlled water, you controlled the county. During the ceremony, the Lanier Raw Water Intake was renamed and dedicated as the Wayne Mason Water Supply Intake Facility.[21] As Gwinnett commissioner Charlotte Nash explained, "What a difference leadership makes. Not only did Wayne Mason recognize the opportunity, he had the courage to take advantage to change the future of Gwinnett for the better and we all benefit, even today, for that."[22]

## Passing the Torch

Perhaps the most important enduring legacy of the Mason family is their commitment to passing the torch. Keith and Tracey Mason have been the two most visible members of the family to take up the baton of public service. Wayne's son, Keith, was born in Snellville, Georgia, on September 20, 1960, the same year John F. Kennedy was elected president. Keith recalled, "My great-grandfather served as sheriff of Gwinnett County in the 1930s and early 1940s, so I grew up around people who are public-spirited and love their community and wanted to see it grow and prosper."[23] Keith recalled an early interest in politics: "In 1966, my uncle

Jimmy ran for the Georgia General Assembly and was elected to serve the county. That was the year Lester Maddox won the governor's race, and I remember coming home from school at the age of six and watching the television to see the results of the governor's race. That was the first time I paid attention to what was going on in politics."[24]

Keith attended elementary and middle school in Gwinnett, graduated from Marist School, and then received his undergraduate and law degrees from the University of Georgia. The first campaign he worked on, outside of those for his uncle or father, was Jimmy Carter's gubernatorial campaign in 1970, when he was a child. He remembered,

> I began to follow politics after the baseball season was over in June. The primary was in September, so I had two months before I went back to school. I volunteered a little for that campaign. Then in 1972, I volunteered for Sam Nunn's senate race, distributing flyers and bumper stickers. The first campaign I was formally involved in was in 1978, when Zell Miller ran for re-election as lieutenant governor. My uncle had introduced me to him four years earlier, and I had accompanied Zell and Shirley Miller on several campaigning trips. Zell was surprised by my knowledge of state issues. I would go on to coordinate Miller's re-election campaign in East Georgia's tenth congressional district and liked to describe him as a maverick from the mountains.[25]

Keith stayed engaged in Georgia politics and served as campaign manager for Zell Miller's run for governor. Keith remembered, "Zell's first official fundraising event was with my dad and supporters in Gwinnett County. We held it in the summer of 1988 at the Marriott Hotel at Gwinnett

Place and raised about $100,000, which was a lot of money back then. He had already accepted some campaign donations, but Zell wanted this to be his first official fundraiser."[26] The Miller campaign headquarters was set up in Virgil Williams's office in Stone Mountain, and Marti Fullerton took a leave of absence from the lieutenant governor's office to work there full time. Through the summer and fall of 1988, the Miller campaign did a poll about creating a state lottery, which would prove to be a very popular and powerful issue. Keith recalled, "It was a populist issue and one that cut across demographic lines. You did not necessarily have to be liberal or conservative to be for a lottery, and support went up when we tied it to education. The combination of those forces is what helped Zell reposition himself in the election."[27]

Zell Miller had introduced lottery legislation in the Georgia General Assembly while still lieutenant governor, realizing that it could help him in the election. It passed the Senate but not the House, and Keith explained that Zell liked the issue politically because it "made his old face look new again. He was in his mid-50s and was very conscious of his long tenure. He did not want his image to be tied to long-serving political figures like Tom Murphy. The lottery was an anti-establishment kind of issue that could really shake things up, and Zell saw the power in that."[28] In January of 1989, the Miller campaign hired James Carville, the well-known political strategist who had been working for Wallace Wilkinson in Kentucky, and who had won on the lottery in 1987, as well as Bob Casey from Pennsylvania and Frank Lautenberg from New Jersey. Keith remembered

> Zell asking [Carville] what he was going to get for the $7,000 a month retainer, to which Carville replied, "I don't sell no matchbooks, no fingernail files, no combs...and I don't go to no Jaycee meetings, and I don't sleep in ratty hotels. All I do is help you come up with and communicate good ideas, and you know there's nothing more powerful than a good idea whose time has come." What Carville did is give Zell confidence to focus on the issues that were important to him and craft a solid message that resonated with voters.[29]

Governor Miller took office in 1991, with Keith as his chief of staff, a role he held until 1993 when Keith became the deputy assistant for Intergovernmental Affairs in President Bill Clinton's White House. This was a major transition, and Keith reflected, "I had been very active on Zell's behalf in the Clinton campaign effort in Georgia and some nationally. I knew their whole team, and I was ready to take on a new challenge. Zell was very supportive, and advised, 'I think you ought to try to go work in the White House. We need somebody up there. I think it would be good for you and for us. I'll put our weight behind it.'"[30] Keith and his family moved to Washington and stayed in that role until 1994, when he came back to Georgia to work for Public Strategies, a public affairs and strategic communications firm headquartered in Austin, Texas. He led their Atlanta office and work with clients such as Atlanta Gas Light, Blue Cross/Blue Shield of Georgia, Coca-Cola, and Eli Lilly. In the summer of 1997, Keith joined the law firm McKenna Long & Aldridge LLP (now Dentons) to take over their government affairs practice when his friend Gordon Giffin left to become ambassador to Canada.

A year after joining the firm, Keith was appointed to the Georgia Ports Authority, coming full circle to join that board the same year his uncle, Jimmy Mason, was killed on a GPA trip to South America. Keith recalled, "Zell and I had talked about me joining the board just as Jimmy was about to rotate off. He died just as I was about to join. I would ultimately serve a year under Miller, four years under Governor Roy Barnes, and nearly three years under Governor Sonny Perdue. I stepped down in 2005, and my friend Bartow Morgan Jr. took my seat, just as the GPA was becoming more involved in land development."[31] Keith stayed at the law firm until 2016, when he established KWM Capital, an investment firm.

Like her cousin Keith, Tracey Mason, Jimmy's daughter, ended up in a life of public service, and she "takes pride in her predecessors' involvement in the county. And growing up in the periphery of their accomplishments is what helped give rise to her own ambitions. She says her father found every opportunity to emulate great values as he worked to make Gwinnett great, but also took time to urge his daughters to flourish into strong, ambitious, independent women." Tracey recalled one particular conversation, in which her father reminded his daughters, "Remember there are three of you. With the divorce rate where it is, statistics say one of you will end up divorced. And even if you don't get divorced, there's no guarantee your husband won't get run over by a train, so you better be ready to take care of yourselves."[32]

Jimmy Mason imparted the same work ethic to Tracey, his eldest daughter, that Wayne did to Keith. Tracey recalled that when she was twelve, "she earned her first one hundred-dollar bill—the summer her uncle [Harvie Ewing] hired her to fill in as a receptionist for a week." She explained, "I thought I'd pass out when I saw it. I'd never laid eyes on a hundred-dollar bill before, and for the longest time, I kept it safe, not having the heart to spend it."[33] She also recalled wanting to drive at the age of sixteen, and her father telling her, "If you're old enough to drive, you're old enough to work." She took it seriously and began working for her uncle. Tracey reflected, "Everything we were taught was taught by action more than by words. It was rarely talked about—it was always modeled." She remembered seeing her father's commitment to public service, which often kept him absent, especially during the legislative session. When she asked him, "'Why do you have to do it, Daddy? Why does it have to be you?,' he'd give me this look and say, 'Somebody with some sense has got to!'"

One of Tracey's earliest memories of her father's commitment to giving to others dates back to when she was in first grade at Snellville Elementary School. While driving her to school, her father asked Tracey about her day.

> We're having a cake walk, and I need a dime to be in it. My dad asked, "What about the kids who don't have a dime?" I don't remember what I said, but I remember him following me into school that day. He spoke with my teacher, Miss Sylvia Martin, and left. When it was time for the cake walk, Miss Sylvia announced to the class that everyone got to participate because Mr. Mason had paid for the whole class. I'm sure that my father would not have asked to take credit, and I would have never known that he'd done that if Miss Sylvia hadn't made that announcement. Examples of his kindnesses to people, individ-

ually and on a larger scale, are too numerous to recount. I know he wouldn't want me to give him credit. After we flew Dr. Charles Woods to Brazil, he was getting ready to operate on my father and asked, "What is his passion?" I didn't hesitate before saying, "His passion is people." Not just the wealthy and well-known people he sometimes associated with, but all people from all walks of life. James Carville told Keith that he valued my father's views in politics because he kept his finger on the pulse of the general public. I think he got his empathic nature from his father, Winston Mason, who was known to pass out business cards after he retired with the following quote on the back: "Do not find fault with the man who limps or stumbles along the road unless you have worn the shoes he wears, or struggled beneath his load. There may be tacks in his shoes that hurt, though hidden away from view, or the burden he bears, placed on your back, might cause you to stumble, too."[34]

Tracey benefitted directly from the growth of Gwinnett as a product of its superior school system, graduating from South Gwinnett High School in 1979. That education afforded her the opportunity to attend the University of North Carolina.

I was working for Webb, Fowler and Tanner [an early Lawrenceville law firm] in high school, and Jones Webb suggested that I apply to UNC. Neither of my parents had finished college, and so I appreciated this guidance. When I received my acceptance, I remember showing Mr. Webb and his telling me, "They don't just give those away, you know." I didn't know because I'd never spent much time away

> from Gwinnett. My father and I visited Chapel Hill that Spring, I decided I wanted to go, and I remember my father walking up to the university's cashier office there and pulling out cash to pay my first semester's tuition. I was surprised that he let me go so far away from home, but he always valued our seeing how other people lived. Of course, he always wanted us to come back home with that knowledge.[35]

After graduating from UNC, Tracey moved to Charlotte, North Carolina, where she worked for Honeywell in their Commercial Construction Division selling microprocessor-based building control systems to the commercial construction industry in the Carolinas. She explained, "I parlayed growing up in the construction and real estate industry into that first job. I give my daddy and Uncle Wayne credit for that and so much more."[36] After starting a family, Tracey moved back to Gwinnett. She stayed home with her two young daughters until it became apparent that she needed to contribute to the family's income. Her father, adding to his earlier encouragement to be self-sufficient, told her then, "'Somebody around here needs to get a job, and you look like the best candidate. You can flip hamburgers, or I'll send you to law school.' I had my doubts because I was thirty years old, had two young children, and had not been in school in eight years or so."[37] But she started law school full time at Georgia State College of Law, was inducted into the legal honor society Phi Delta Phi, and worked in the tax clinic there.

Tracey started her career with Andersen, Davidson and Tate in Lawrenceville working primarily in their real estate and land use divisions. In 2000, she went out on her own and developed a solo practice, taking cases at first from contemporaries of her father and uncle who valued her connections and who hired her to pursue land use issues. She explained, "It meant a lot to me to always maintain some aspect of my practice in real estate. Folks in that world especially would remember my father to me after he died, and it kept me in my uncle Wayne's world."[38] Her practice later expanded to include work as a mediator and arbitrator as well as a guardian ad litem in Gwinnett's probate and superior courts, protecting the interests of children and the elderly. She was later appointed by the City of Duluth as a municipal court judge. In the family tradition, she has always been active in the Gwinnett community. Tracey is a graduate of Leadership Gwinnett, and her community endeavors include serving as president of the Gwinnett Rotary Club and the Community Foundation for Northeast Georgia. She has chaired the Cancer Ball for the American Cancer Society in Gwinnett as well as the Button Gwinnett Tribute for the Council for Quality Growth. She has served on numerous boards in Gwinnett, including the Gwinnett Chamber of Commerce, the Council for Quality Growth, the United Way, the Gwinnett Coalition for Health and Human Services, Annandale Village, and Friends of Gwinnett Senior Services. Tracey cofounded the Women's Initiative for United Way in Gwinnett. She is a member of the Gwinnett County Bar Association, the State Bar of Georgia, and the American Bar Association. After more than two decades working closely with the people of Gwinnett as an attorney and also serving her community as a volunteer, Tracey was elected in 2018 as a Gwinnett County Superior Court judge, where she continues to serve. Aware of her power, she stated, "You want to make sure you do the right thing for every person who stands before you. I have a lot of responsibility, but I also have a lot of people bolstering and holding me up. I've got a village that includes lifelong friends, respected colleagues, former clients, and many generations of family buried in Gwinnett soil, so I feel lifted up and sustained." She recalls the impact of her father, whom she lost too soon when he was only sixty-one. "I hear him in my mind on my best days, every day. I hear him, and I hope the best of me comes out, because that's what he'd want."[39]

While Keith and Tracey hold the most public roles in the Mason family today, other family members have contributed behind the scenes. As Keith explained,

> I have three sisters who are not public figures, but they are still very much engaged with their community. One sister, Kim, nearest to me in age, has been active in philanthropy with her husband around Catholic-related causes and healthcare, supporting Holy Spirit Catholic School and Piedmont Hospital. Her father-in-law and my father were partners in the Braselton land deal years ago. My middle sister Kay's husband, Tim Hamil, has been a judge for many years and is now chief judge for Gwinnett County. My youngest sister, Kristy's husband, Dan English, has served on the Gwinnett Public Library Board of Trustees.[40]

Tracey's two sisters, Teresa Mason Waters and Tina Mason Carico, also live private lives. Teresa and her husband, Gary, now married for more than forty years, were high school sweethearts, and like her parents, had two children, and now have three grandchildren. They have a multigenerational landscaping business that they have owned and operated for more than thirty years, having had nurseries in Grayson and Braselton along with a tree farm in Hartwell. Dr. Tina Mason Carico practiced obstetrics and gynecology in Gwinnett, beginning by sharing space with her cousin, Dr. Miles Mason III, and continued practicing for decades before turning her attention to her family with husband David Carico and their son, the youngest grandchild, James Mason Carico. Taken together, the Masons continue to contribute to a range of areas throughout the county that they have so long called home.

# Chapter 8

# Dynamic and Diverse

> "I think diversity is the best thing that has ever happened to us."—Wayne Mason

The Mason family has had a significant impact on the growth and development of their home county in a variety of areas and helped lay the groundwork for its transformation into one of the most diverse and fastest growing counties in the country. Wayne once said, "The county had major problems, and I didn't know all the answers. But one thing that we had when I was on the commission was a core group of people who had a unity of purpose. These people are no longer around. Much has changed in Gwinnett since I was a child, and I think diversity is the best thing that has ever happened to us."[1] Understanding Gwinnett in the twenty-first century requires a look back to the political, demographic, and economic landscape of the 1980s.

## The Changing Political Landscape

The 1980s not only brought explosive growth to Gwinnett, but also reflected the changing political landscape that had rippled through the region since the 1960s. As Bill Kirby explains, "The almost complete takeover of Gwinnett in the mid-1980s by the Republican Party was stunning and complete. Since Barry Goldwater's 1964 campaign for president, Republicans had been gaining strength in the Sunbelt. The issues change, but the South remains conservative. For more than a century that conservative banner had been carried by Georgia's Democratic Party."[2] Many historians look to President Lyndon B. Johnson's signing of the Civil Rights Act of 1964 as a watershed moment. Bill Moyers, who was the White House press secretary from 1965 to 1967, recalled Johnson's melancholy mood after signing the landmark legislation. According to Moyers, Johnson was aware of the political risk and said, "I think we just delivered the South to the Republican Party for a long time."[3] He was not wrong.

Until World War II, the Democratic Party dominated political life in the South. But that was about to change. When President Harry Truman brought a civil rights platform to the 1948 Democratic National Convention, a group of delegates, later named the "Dixiecrats," left and held a separate convention. In opposition to their party, they nominated segregationist Strom Thurmond on a "States' Rights Democratic Party" ticket. Thurmond eventually lost to Truman—but not before he carried four Southern states (South Carolina, Alabama, Louisiana, and Mississippi). David Goldfield, writing in *The Gifted Generation: When Government Was Good*, explained that it was "the first time since before the Civil War that the South was not solidly Democratic."[4]

Gwinnett's demographics played a role in this change. As historian James Cobb argues, "At the midpoint of the 20th century, Gwinnett, 30 miles northeast of Atlanta, was largely rural, with just 32,000 inhabitants, more than 95% of them white. Scarcely 2% of the residents had completed four years of college, and only 25% of the workforce held professional or managerial jobs." [5] These demographic changes were reflected in the political map. As Bill Kirby observes,

> But things changed rapidly with the presidential election of Ronald Reagan in 1980. The old Southerners began to stop thinking about themselves as Democrats. And by the time Reagan sought re-election in 1984, a majority of Gwinnett voters put the Grand Old Party candidates into local offices. That election year, not a single Democrat either achieved or retained office if his or her office was located solely in the county.[6]

This was a dramatic change from just a decade before. As Atlanta's white population shrank in the 1960s and 1970s, Gwinnett's grew. By 1990, 357,000 people lived in Gwinnett, and nine out of ten of them were white while an increasingly large number of them voted Republican, like much of the rest of the South.[7]

But this was not the end of the story. Gwinnett was becoming a destination for African American residents looking to relocate to the South from other parts of the country. In the 1990s, the black population doubled. In the next decade, it increased by 140 percent while white residents moved further out to Barrow and Walton Counties. By 2020, more than 30 percent of Gwinnett's population was black.[8] Latino residents also found Gwinnett a welcoming place. Many moved from Texas and Louisiana as employment in oilfields dried up. The explosive growth in foreign-owned companies also helped attract Asian residents, and by

2020, 13 percent of the county population was of Asian descent. Not everyone was happy about the change. By 2007, Gwinnett became a majority non-white county, but those changes were not reflected in the county commission and board of education until 2018. While Gwinnett could be counted on to reliably vote Republican since 1984, it had shifted to supporting Democrats Barack Obama and Hillary Clinton in 2012 and 2016, respectively.[9] A lifelong supporter of the Democratic Party, Wayne used to quip "I'm a Democrat since I don't have enough money to be a Republican."

## The Power of Diversity

In his article "From Burbs to Pueblo: Mass Immigration and Gwinnett County's Demographic Revolution, 1990 to 2020," Marko Maunula argues that

> the story of Gwinnett County offers a microcosmic encapsulation of the economic and demographic development of the post-World War II South.... Economic modernization and white flight fueled suburbanization and further contributed to the size, scope, and speed of the transformation, as Gwinnett rapidly evolved from a southern community with a strong sense of place to a modern, globally connected, and continuously transforming community.[10]

By 2018, more than 25 percent of county residents had been born outside of the United States, a far cry from what Wayne and Jimmy Mason experienced as they were building their businesses after World War II. Sometimes referred to as a mini-Ellis Island, Gwinnett's growth is due to a number of factors. Between 1970 and 2017, immigrants to the United States grew from 9.6 to 44.5 million.[11] As a result,

> it is hard to overestimate the size and scope of Georgia's demographic transformation over the last five decades. In the 1960s, Georgia's story was still predominately Black and white, and the state's story was almost always told with a deep southern accent. The Sunbelt boom had begun, but it was still searching for its momentum. Atlanta remained a southern town, with surrounding counties that in many ways continued to hold on to their rural character. The metropolitan region was still locked in a fight with Birmingham, Alabama, for the role of the South's leading city.[12]

These evolving demographics changed everything—housing, schools, work patterns, transportation. Maunula argues,

> A look at the numbers reveals that the bulk of the immigration to Georgia took place during the late stages of the Sunbelt boom. The biggest change occurred during the 1990s, with immigration to the state remaining substantial after the new millennium but its growth somewhat tempered. Additionally, by 2017 these new immigrants came overwhelmingly from Latin America (48.1 percent) and Asia (30.1 percent), as those two regions easily surpassed Western Europe and Canada as the most common home regions of Georgia-bound immigrants.[13]

There was great excitement for the changes, mainly from the business community. As Nick Masino, president and CEO of the Gwinnett Chamber of Commerce explained, "We do a new member orientation every eight weeks, and it looks like the mosaic of people in Gwinnett County. All races, religions, creeds, and colors are represented, and it's great."[14] Former Gwinnett County Commission chair Charlotte Nash agreed: "I see a bright future for Gwinnett. We've got a great chamber of commerce and economic development staff in Partnership Gwinnett, plus a strong business community and great cities in addition to the county itself. There are a lot of good things to look forward to, and I expect Gwinnett County will continue to be attractive to families."[15] Businessman Benjamin Rincon sees the same kind of opportunity. In 2005, he worked to remake the Santa Fe Mall in Duluth, a two-story facility that had opened in the 1980s, into a new kind of commercial space, one that includes the Spanish-language radio station La Que Bueno (101.9) and a twelve-screen movie theater. As *The Atlantic* reports, "The sound of Latin music and aromas from Congas Express food stand immediately greet visitors to the colorful and bustling mall."[16] Today, the mall is a destination that has a tax clinic and travel and salon services plus a giant playground and hosts concerts featuring artists like Banda Renovacion, Los Reyes de America, Polo Urias, La Apuesta, and Alejandra Rojas. Madelyn A., writing on the review site Yelp, explained, "I actually felt like I was walking through the Mercado in Mexico. It was very nice to see that they have actually grown and added more stores and services to support this community."[17]

While some welcomed the changes, not everyone was enthusiastic. Longtime residents often look to the past with longing. Tyler Estep, writing for the *Atlanta Journal-Constitution*, explains,

> When Dan Franklin was growing up in the 1950s and '60s, the Duluth area—and the rest of Gwinnett County, for that matter—was farmland and simple living. It was a few thousand folks spread out across 400-something square miles northeast of Atlanta. Just about everyone knew each other, and just about everyone was white. None of that is the case any longer, not by a long shot. Gwinnett is a booming suburb with one of the most diverse communities in the Southeastern United States. And Franklin, who moved from Davenport Road to another part of Gwinnett decades ago, admits he sometimes feels like a stranger in a county where he's lived for all 65 years of his life.... For many longtime Gwinnett residents, the majority of whom are white, the county's almost simultaneous explosion in size and diversity can be a difficult thing to reckon with. In some, that reckoning can manifest itself as racism, but it can also be a different sort of thing—a longing for the South, the home, that they grew up with.[18]

It is not unusual that such a dramatic demographic change would generate a range of responses.

Maunula argues, "The development has not been without its challenges. As the county grew and its demographic profile changed, some white people decided to abandon Gwinnett County. In the early 2000s Gwinnett lost 40,000 white residents, while it gained 107,000 African Americans, 97,000 Hispanics, and 43,000 Asian residents."[19] These divides were reflected in the 2016 presidential election, where many native-born white residents supported Donald Trump and reflected JoAnn Weather's sentiment: "There used to be a place where we could go out to eat and get Southern cooking."[20] But the county overall voted

Democratic, and the 2018 governor's race "demonstrated the county's continued shift, as the Democratic candidate, Stacey Abrams, bested the Republican—and eventual winner—Brian Kemp by more than fourteen percentage points."[21]

A story about Pedro "Pete" Marin from 2003 illustrates the tensions in the county. As *The Atlantic* reported, "Three days after being sworn in as the first Latino state legislator in Georgia's history, Pedro Marin had an ethics complaint filed against him. It said that he was a 'Mexican federal government agent infiltrated in the Georgia General Assembly.' There were a couple of problems with that charge: 1) Marin is Puerto Rican; 2) He's never been to Mexico." Marin reflected on the incident: "It was a wake-up call for me. There's this anti-immigrant group out there with this new wave of Latinos, and we've got to be more aware."[22] Marin has gone on to have a distinguished career representing District 96 for twenty years and has been active on a range of committees including Banks and Banking, Economic Development and Tourism, and Industry and Labor.[23] Gwinnett is not the only county in the state or nation that is facing these kinds of growing pains.

## Looking to the Future

Significant change often brings a range of complications. In 2009, a controversy regarding a zoning dispute over building a new worship center for the Dar-e 'Abbas mosque in Lilburn is one such issue. The mosque, which had operated in a 2,000-square-foot building on 1.4 acres for ten years at the intersection of US Highway 29 and Hood Road, applied in 2009 to purchase 6.5 acres of land to build a larger mosque, cemetery, parking area, and gymnasium.[24] The controversy that erupted made national news and suggested that Gwinnett had a reputation for religious intolerance. Diana Preston, a Lilburn resident since the 1970s, was mayor during the controversy, and explained in 2011, "I still get emails from outside of the state about it, from California, Wisconsin, all over. It's like, 'Good grief.' This has been really unfortunate."[25] Preston was planning to sell family land to help build the 20,000-square-foot worship center. The resulting controversy generated a Department of Justice investigation for discrimination. Just a cursory glance at some of the mosque-opposition emails reveals the implicit bias and racism: one email said, "Remember the World Trade Center and what these people stand for," while another said, "By letting these people having [*sic*] a Mosque built is only a stepping stone to possible future disasters."[26] The city incurred more than a hundred thousand dollars in legal fees, and the incident reflected deep divisions in the city and county. As Preston explained, "I think everybody thinks of the old times as better times—and sometimes when you really drill down into it, they weren't really better times."[27]

The mosque controversy illustrates the challenges of rapid change and the undercurrent of religious intolerance that has shaped the South for centuries. Around this same time, there were similar controversies regarding the Mississippi Muslim Association (Madison, MS) in 2009, the Islamic Center of Tennessee and the Islamic Center of Murfreesboro (in Antioch and Murfreesboro, TN, respectively) in 2010, the Islamic Center of North Fulton and the Hamzah Islamic Center (both in Alpharetta, GA) in 2011 and 2012, the Islamic Center of Longview (TX) in 2012, and the Islamic Center of Richmond (VA) in 2012. But this particular issue is not confined to the South. In 2012, the Pew Research Center published "Controversies Over Mosques and Islamic Centers Across the U.S.," which presented an interactive map showing "53 proposed mosques and Islamic centers that have encountered community resistance in recent years." These controversies sprang up in dozens of communities, from California and Illinois to Wisconsin and Maine. While some concerns concentrated on issues like traffic, noise, and parking, others focused on "fears about Islam, sharia law, and terrorism."[28]

The mosque was not the only issue related to diversity that Gwinnett has faced in recent years. As reported in the *Atlanta Journal-Constitution*, "In August 2016, the Georgia Association of Elected Officials and the Georgia NAACP filed a lawsuit challenging the way Gwinnett County's commission and school board districts are drawn. The county has never had a non-white member on either entity, and the groups allege that their district maps were drawn specifically to thwart the voice of minority voters."[29] This certainly looked to be the case, and a new map was developed to reflect the demographic reality of the county. In 2016, Sam Park became the first Asian American Democrat elected to the legislature, and soon the county was almost completely Democratic, a significant shift from the previous decades. In 2018, Marlene Fosque became the first African American member of the Gwinnett County Commission, and by 2020, the entire commission was comprised of people of color. But the change was not embraced by everyone, and Republicans in the Georgia General Assembly tried to eliminate the new redistricting map and submit one of their own. Representative Bonnie Rich, one of the last Republicans in the legislature from Gwinnett, explained their rationale: "My constituents come to me, and they tell me they have no seat at the table."[30] Rich's comments do not address the fact that diverse residents in Gwinnett had no representation in the past. Michael Li, of the Brennan Center for Justice, explained, "Untangling race and politics is one of the hardest things courts get asked to do, and it's particularly hard in the south where race and politics overlap to a very large degree." Eventually, Governor Brian Kemp, a Republican, accepted the newly drawn maps that were expressly drawn to solidify Republican majorities, prompting a number of legal challenges that are still pending.[31] While Gwinnett has become a minority-majority county, this has not yet translated into actual voting power, an issue that will likely dominate the region for years to come.

The issues surrounding the mosque and redistricting suggest that Gwinnett's transformation from a sleepy agricultural county to part of a major metropolis reflects the same kinds of growing pains experienced by many suburban counties. But there is reason for optimism. As Wayne Mason explained, "I feel the diversity of people in Gwinnett is a big plus for us. It's the best thing that has happened to Gwinnett. We ought to recognize that all everyone wants...is to have safe streets and a better life for their family. If I were young again today, I would want to have children in the public schools and learn to speak Spanish."[32] His niece Tracey Mason echoes that sentiment: "Demographically, Gwinnett has changed a lot from when I was growing up. But I love the diversity and the different cultures I see around us today, even at the courthouse, and I love hearing the different stories people share about who they are and where they came from and how they got to Gwinnett."[33]

# Epilogue

## The World According to Wayne

"I have had a great life, and I would do it all again."
—Wayne Mason

When asked about what constitutes success, Wayne Mason offered a nuanced answer:

> I never really said to myself—now I'm successful. After all, how do you measure that? Financially, generally, we did very well, but we also had plenty of ups and downs. I think there are other, equally important, ways to measure success. For instance, look at your family, your wife and children. I have been married for more than sixty years and have four great children, eleven grandchildren, and five great-grandchildren. We are a close-knit group, and I think that is really important. I also live in a great community, am still active, and have lots of friends. I am still working in my 80s and love it. Maybe that's success—a good family, interesting work, a good system of support.[1]

Wayne's most enduring partnership is with his wife, Ann. He often says

> I was successful because she helped make everything run smoothly behind the scenes. She did so much to create a wonderful home and help raise our four children. We were engaged in our community and

> church, and she liked to say, "Behind every successful man is a woman pushing him to do his best." I know it's not easy to be the spouse of a public figure. She took a lot of abuse with patience and grace. My success is largely due to her strength and support.[2]

Woven into Wayne's story are important life lessons that emerged in the writing of this book that can be applied to any aspect of your life.

LIFE LESSON #1: Live below your means. This advice seems obvious but often goes unheeded. Wayne likes to say "I can't tell the difference when I'm broke and when I've got millions. I don't change my lifestyle. I've lived in the same house.... I drive the same car, wear the same clothes, eat the same food, go to the same church, associate with the same people I went to high school with. I don't make money to change friends."[3] It did not matter if he was doing well or close to bankruptcy, he controlled his spending, saved, and invested wisely. He also stuck to his mantra "always outgrow your capital."

It is easy to think you need to buy the newest car, boat, or iPhone, and our society rewards constant consumerism with things like planned obsolescence. Long gone are the days when you kept your house for thirty years and drove a car over 200,000 miles. The Federal Reserve Bank of New York reported an increase in the total amount of debt in the American household, which rose by $27 billion to $15.85 trillion in the first quarter of 2022. Journalist Megan DeMatteo reported on CNBC on November 18, 2021, that "the average American has $90,460 in debt."[4] The article goes on to show how much debt each generation has accumulated, and it is alarming: Gen Z ($9,593), millennials

($78,396), Gen X ($135,841), baby boomers ($96,984), and the Silent Generation, or those over seventy-five years old ($40,925). The most common forms of debt seem to be credit cards, automobile loans, mortgage loans, personal loans, student loans, and, finally, home equity lines of credit. It is hard to build any wealth when you are paying high interest rates. One way to avoid debt is to pay for things in cash. That will make you more aware of how you spend your money.

Nationwide Insurance has a personal finance section on their website that offers a troubling statistic: "If you can't cover your current lifestyle and all your bills with after-tax income, you're not living within your means. Without enough savings, many adults live paycheck to paycheck, which means they don't have enough money for emergency expenses. A study done by the Federal Reserve (PDF) showed that 44% of adults say they couldn't pay for a $400 emergency expense, or they would need to borrow money or sell something to pay for it."[5] There are dozens of articles published each month, from the *Wall Street Journal* to *Money*, that focus on the importance of sound financial habits, offering key takeaways like

> living below your means can help you improve your financial health and prioritize goals like saving and investing. You can take steps to live below your means, like budgeting and finding ways to reduce spending. Finding ways to pay down debt can help you save on interest charges so you can keep more money in your wallet. Evaluating your current financial habits and being conscious of any changes to your budget can help you stay on track.[6]

Add to that Wayne's insistence on diversification and the lessons on hard work and frugality inherited from his parents and passed down to his children and grandchildren and you have a recipe for success.

LIFE LESSON #2: Find out what you are good at and do a lot more of it. At the age of twelve, Wayne's father gave him $10, and he never took any money from him again. He was an extrovert and loved talking to people and has started more businesses than you can count. As a child, he made wreaths and sold eggs; as a businessman, he maintained upwards of twelve businesses at the same time and invested widely in real estate. Even in his eighties, Wayne is still going strong. "I'm going to die doing my last deal. I mean I love it. I don't play golf. I'll go hunting once or twice a year, but mostly I'm going because there's somebody I want to be around and we're doing some kind of deal. But other than that, I'm a dealaholic. I want to do a deal every day."[7]

But following your passion has some caveats. As Dan Cable argues in *Harvard Business Review*, "When it comes to career advice, 'Follow your passion!' is a little like 'Follow your bliss!' Sure, passion sounds like a wonderful thing when choosing where to invest your time and effort. After all, the average person spends more than 90,000 hours at work in their lifetime. Yes, that is one-third of your entire life. So, of course it would be nice if that time was spent doing something you actually love."[8] The article then goes on to pose an alternative way to look at work and success, positing that you should "follow your blisters" and instead consider that work that might be fulfilling is about "perseverance and struggling through tasks even though they are not always blissful." Cable clarifies, "The things that always seem to get done often reveal insight into what will fulfill you in your career—they are the things we never need to be asked twice to do, and ultimately, they are more satisfying than the things we may love to do largely because they come natural and easy to us."[9]

Lauren Howe, John Jachimowicz, and Jochen Menges make a similar argument in their article "Your Job Doesn't Have to be Your Passion." Loving the news or nature might lead you to jobs in journalism or the National Park Service, but long hours living in remote or dangerous circumstances and difficulty maintaining a work-life balance can make these professions undesirable. The authors instead argue that passion is one factor, but asking probing questions can offer a more realistic perspective: "Do I need to pursue my passion through my work? What would it look like to pursue this passion outside of work? Would it be equally fulfilling?"[10] Focusing solely on passion has the disadvantage of burnout. "Some research suggests that transforming hobbies into work could undermine your enjoyment of these activities, as your interest gets sapped by the pursuit of external rewards like compensation."[11] Wayne's approach to business and real estate was not driven exclusively by his love for construction and land ownership, but rather motivated by his recognition that he had a cluster of skills—relationship-building, negotiation, and forecasting—that were personally fulfilling and helped him contribute to his community. For Wayne, that was the key to success.

LIFE LESSON #3: Diversify, diversify, diversify. Wayne had plenty of ups and downs but always stayed afloat because of the broad diversification of his businesses. When the real estate market bottomed out during the recession, his liquor stores kept him solvent. Those two stores sold for more than $30 million dollars. It is also important to get your money to work for you. Wayne tells a story about his grandfather giving him fifty cents when he was a child. Then he told him to loan it back to him with the promise of paying five cents interest. He recalled that this exchange was an early lesson in economics. You have to invest, and Wayne found out early that real estate was a path to real success. If you own land, you can always get money. But in a recession, that can become a problem, as Wayne explained: "You can't take a five-dollar bucket of dirt to buy groceries."[12] That's why land can't be your only investment. You have to have multiple income streams to plan for the unexpected. If the housing market slows down, the funeral home, tile store, or liquor store might be profitable. Don't depend too much on one thing.

Writing for *Entrepreneur*, Lisa Song Sutton offers a range of perspectives from readers on this very topic. One explained,

> My business portfolio is wide and varied: food and beverage, real estate, shipping and ecommerce. The 2020 pandemic was the ultimate justification in my business diversification. My food business took a massive hit as tourism temporarily came to a screeching halt due to government-mandated shutdowns. In contrast, for as hard hit as Sin City Cupcakes was, shipping, real estate, and ecommerce had their best years. People started home-based ecommerce businesses, and they fled high-tax states to move to Nevada. Had I not been diversified and had solely relied

on just one business as my main stream of income, I would have been in a world of trouble.[13]

The article goes on to offer advice from multiple industries and suggests subscribing to newsletters, blogs, and Listservs like "Contrarian Thinking" that offer new business opportunities, discussions about trends, and business models that include starting side hustles to help hedge against economic downturns.

LIFE LESSON #4: Give back. If you have become successful and have something to share, do it. The Masons have always been engaged in the community, and Wayne often donates money to causes without saying anything about it. He gave the land to Snellville to build Briscoe Park and then made sure it was named for the mayor, and he donated land to Crosspoint Baptist Church. He is especially proud of the athletic facilities he helped build at E. R. Snell Field. Wayne has spent much of his life asking a simple question: What does my community need? Then he dedicated himself to making that happen—whether it was a water system for Gwinnett while on the county commission or donating land for recreation. Wayne likes to say "you don't want to be a taker. You want to help build your community. Our companies used to sponsor between eight and ten Little League teams. That way all the kids could play, and it looked like the whole community was engaged in helping them. I got so much more of a thrill giving my money away than I ever did in making it."[14]

Eric Barvin, founder and CEO of Barvin, a property management and investment company, argues that giving back is both professionally and personally satisfying. Writing in *Forbes*, he explains, "Many business leaders tend to focus on the bottom line rather than giving back to the community—especially in economic turbulence. But giving back is an investment not only in the community but also in long-term goals and core values. I believe companies whose values and mission are centered around the community can be the most successful and withstand the test of time."[15] Giving and community service also have very practical personal benefits. The Cleveland Clinic shows that research in this area indicates that giving is good for your health. Dr. Susan Albers argues, "When we do things for other people, it makes us feel much more engaged and joyful. That's good for our health and our happiness."[16] Public service and philanthropy help lower blood pressure, extend your lifespan, reduce stress, and promote a "helper's high," which "boosts self-esteem, elevates happiness, and combats feelings of depression."[17]

LIFE LESSON #5: Invest in people because relationships matter. The most important lesson Wayne Mason learned is that everything is based on relationships, and your reputation is as good as gold. He explained,

> You will not be successful in any arena—politics, business, philanthropy—if you don't cultivate strong relationships and invest in the people around you. You have to be trusted and reliable. My word was my bond. If I said I was going to do something, I did it. I made a lot of million-dollar deals on a handshake and nothing else. I remember Herman Russell and I were looking at a deal. We talked about the details, and he sent me the check for $150,000 because we trusted each other. I don't remember signing anything. It was just a gentleman's agreement. I just gave him my word, and he gave me his. When the deal

> fell through, I sent him the money back. I did a lot of business on a handshake.[18]

Wayne is an eternal optimist: "I believe that you can do anything with the right people. Sometimes it doesn't work out, but I think you get more winners than losers. People want to do the right thing. And if it doesn't work out, so be it. I see people all the time who owe me money, but I don't feel bitter. It's just the cost of doing business."[19]

Fostering positive relationships is the key to success in business, as Tina Hovsepian, writing in *Forbes*, explains: "As one of my mentors has always expressed to me, behind every business there are people, and people function in society via relationships. Therefore, successful business is built on good relationships. I am a firm believer in this philosophy, as it has only served me well along my journey as a founder."[20] She goes on to argue that you need to cultivate relationships with four key constituents: vendors and consultants; employees; partners; and, finally, clients, members, and their customers. To do that, you need to work on three areas: expressing appreciation, good communication, and realistic deadlines and goals. She concludes her article with, "It is amazing how a bit of a personal touch can go a long way. Companies who embrace this culture are more successful. If you don't believe me, just take a look at the list of the top companies to work for and find out why they are on top."[21]

LIFE LESSON #6: Conflict breeds conflict. Wayne had a rule that he would never sue anybody. In his business career, he had plenty of people who failed to fulfill a contract, but he learned to write it off and move beyond the issue. Otherwise, he explains, "all you do is pay lawyers and end up tangled up in lawsuits that sap your time and energy."[22] There is a lot of research to back up that perspective, as Mike Myatt argues in "Five Keys of Dealing with Workplace Conflict." He explains, "The ability to recognize conflict, understand the nature of conflict, and to be able to bring swift and just resolution to conflict will serve you well as a leader—the inability to do so may well be your downfall." Myatt explains that most conflicts come from one of two issues—ineffective communication or allowing emotions to drive decisions. Successful leaders employ variations of his advice. They define acceptable behavior to avoid confusion or mismanaged expectations. They are proactive and address conflict directly, thus preventing issues from spiraling out of control. They understand that WIIFM (What's In It For Me) factor and understand what motivates clients, their employees, or partners. Finally, they pick their battles. The latter suggestion has been the key to Wayne's success. He could easily have become embroiled in lengthy legal disputes over contracts but often decided instead to walk away and look for new opportunities. This approach is the fifth piece of Myatt's advice—view conflict as an opportunity. When faced with a dilemma, consider asking where we might learn, grow, and develop strategically. Turning the other cheek and showing compromise, compassion, and grace can go a long way in promoting a healthy business and a happy life.

LIFE LESSON #7: Cheerlead, don't micromanage. From raising children to supporting employees, Wayne always prized self-sufficiency. Keith Mason remembered,

> My dad never told any of his children what they should do...he was always a quiet backer, but he was

> never one to micromanage his children in their lives. He was more of a cheerleader than a micromanager. He always supported everything I did but he never said to me, "you need to do this, not that." He would answer questions and provide advice...but he wanted you to do what you wanted to do.[23]

Wayne liked to explain it this way: "Kids are like water. You have to let them set their own level. You can't impose on them what you think they ought to be doing. Let them start working early, so they learn the value of labor. Set up a bank account for them, so they can learn the value of money. Expect a lot of them and they will rise to the occasion."[24]

This advice applies to the business world as well. Rebecca Knight argues that you should ask three questions when leading a team to avoid becoming a micromanager: "What can you do to give your people the space they need to succeed and learn? How should you prioritize what matters? And how do you get comfortable stepping back?"[25] Amy Jen Su and Muriel Maignan Wilkins, coauthors of *Own the Room*, discuss the problem: "Micromanaging dents your team's morale by establishing a tone of mistrust—and it limits your team's capacity to grow."[26] Failure to recognize that having autonomy is an essential human need has the potential to undermine judgement, expertise, and confidence. Paul Jones, writing for the *Milwaukee Journal Sentinel*, explains why cheerleading is a better approach: "Esprit de corps is a good thing. Building strong morale is an important part of building a winning team, on the battlefield, on the playing field and in business. And cheerleading can be a worthwhile part of plans for building esprit de corps. Celebrating high performance is a good way to encourage high performance, and encouraging high performance is, finally, the ultimate objective of cheerleaders."[27]

LIFE LESSON #8: Take risks early and often. Business success often depends on taking big risks. One of Wayne's biggest was in 1965 when he bought most of the land in downtown Snellville. Still young in his career, he spent $100,000 and bought eleven tracts of land, including the cemetery. Wayne explained,

> That was a lot of money back then, and I needed to borrow it, so I went to see Bartow Morgan Sr. at Brand Bank. I told him what I had done, and he said he'd go see the land when the bank closed that day. I showed it all to him and he said, "Wayne, that's a hell of a deal, but it's not something we usually do. But my mother might lend you the money." So, I went to see her, and she gave me a loan for seven percent interest. It took me about a year to pay it off. I gave some of the land to the Baptist church and sold some to American Oil for $25,000. In the end, I made hundreds of thousands of dollars, but it was a big risk, and I needed help to do it right.[28]

Wayne often said "I look back on my career, and I've been up and down. I've made money and lost it—over and over again. But you have to take chances and risks in business. My theory has always been the same—I can't lose anything because I never had anything else to start with."[29]

Justin Grome, the founder of Clonefluence Inc., argues that risk-taking is essential to entrepreneurship. While 70 percent of startups fail in their first ten years, the ones that make it have the potential to transform entire industries. Risk-taking, while often fraught with fear and uncertainty, has clear benefits.

There are countless advantages that taking risks has to offer. Entrepreneurs may find a certain strategy that works for them that no one else has taken advantage of because of the significant risk involved. If you succeed in something new, then you find a strategy in your niche that works without any competitors willing to do the same, at least for a while. In my experience, companies only tend to succeed if they try new ways to build that no one else has already tried. In general, trying new things in life is a must to explore all avenues and have a sense of what is out there.[30]

This is the lesson that Wayne learned early on in his career, and it has served him well.

LIFE LESSON #9: It all comes down to character. Leadership means different things to different people, but for the Masons, the focus has always been on putting your community's interests above your own. Their public service always had an emphasis on the service part. Wayne served on the Gwinnett County Commission from 1972 to 1980 and made building the infrastructure of the county his main priority. He never intended to be a professional politician and was not concerned with building a power base or empire. He ran for public office to see if he could help solve big problems. Once it became clear what was needed, he focused all of his energy on building roads, water systems, and sewers. During his tenure, he refused to take a credit card from the county. He paid all of his expenses, regardless of what they were, out of his own pocket. As he often says,

"Either you have character, or you don't. There is no middle ground."

Character is at the heart of everything Wayne Mason does, and it is often the key to success in business. Ulrik Juul Christensen writes, in "Why Character May be the Secret Ingredient for Future Success," that character is a "timeless virtue" that has real-world application. He quotes Angela Duckworth, author of *Grit: The Power of Passion and Perseverance* and cofounder of CharacterLab, who thinks about character as "everything we do to help other people as well as ourselves." In this context, she identifies three features: "strength of heart," including gratitude to support relationships; "strength of will," such as grit and self-control to propel achievement; and "strength of mind," or curiosity for independent thinking.[31] The strength of heart, will, and mind sums up the world according to Wayne Mason.

If you asked Wayne to look back on his eighty-plus years to think about what he might have done differently, he always says nothing. His niece, Tracey Mason, concurs: "One of the things I admire most about my uncle Wayne is that he changes with the times. He is a visionary, often sees changes coming, but, whether he does or not, he embraces change and makes the most of it. At the same time, he never forgets where he came from. I've seen that in him over my lifetime, and it is indeed remarkable."[32] Wayne's wife, Ann, reflects on his legacy: "He has loved Gwinnett his whole life and always kept the county's benefit close to his heart. If it was good for Gwinnett, he was for it. He has always been very creative and tried to come up with good solutions. He really helped shape the county and the state."[33] Jim Henderson shares a similar sentiment: "The Masons' legacy can be found in their work ethic. I never saw Jimmy or Wayne sitting still. They were always trying to accomplish something. Their father, Winston, was the same way. I think you see that with the next generation as well. They never stop, they are always moving, always getting things done."[34]

Wayne not only witnessed the dramatic changes in Gwinnett County, he and his family were also responsible for many of them. As *Gwinnett Magazine* reported, Wayne Mason has "made a lot of deals, built a lot of homes, met a lot of people, inked a lot of contracts, worked more jobs, and started more businesses than you could imagine. Whether he was selling eggs in wealthy Atlanta neighborhoods or making decisions that would benefit Gwinnett County residents for generations to come, the young man from south Gwinnett has one thing about him that remains unchanged.... It's still hard to keep up with Wayne Mason."[35]

# NOTES

[1] "Tribute to Wayne Mason," *Congressional Record* (Senate), March 16, 2015, S1526-7. https://www.congress.gov/114/crec/2015/03/16/CREC-2015-03-16-pt1-PgS1526-3.pdf. Accessed April 1, 2022.

[2] Andy Ambrose, "Atlanta," *New Georgia Encyclopedia*, last modified June 8, 2022. https://www.georgiaencyclopedia.org/articles/counties-cities-neighborhoods/atlanta/. Accessed October 1, 2021.

[3] Wayne Mason, interview by Catherine Lewis, March 23, 2021. The Mason-Todd House is one of the oldest homes in Snellville, Georgia, dating from the nineteenth century.

[4] Ibid.

[5] Curt Yeomans, "Progress: Gwinnett County's Story from 1818 to 2018 is One of Growth and Change," *Gwinnett Daily Post*, February 25, 2018.

[6] Kathryn Nikolich, "Gwinnett County, Georgia, A Sunbelt Community: The Invention of a Postwar Suburb," Master's thesis, Georgia State University, January 16, 2015, 8.

*Chapter 1: The Beginnings*

[1] Button Gwinnett was born in 1753 in England and came to Savannah as a child in 1765. He struggled as a merchant, and, according to historian Stan Deaton, "he purchased St. Catherines Island and set himself up as a planter. He became active in local politics, winning election to the Commons House of Assembly. By 1773, Gwinnett was again in financial straits; he sold most of his personal property and possessions and withdrew from the political scene." He reemerged as a political figure during the Revolutionary War and signed the Declaration of Independence with fellow Georgians George Walton and Lyman Hall. Gwinnett was involved in Georgia's Provincial Congress and in a failed military action in British East Florida, which put him in conflict with Lachlan McIntosh, who fatally shot him in a duel. Stan Deaton, "Button Gwinnett," *New Georgia Encyclopedia* (last modified August 1, 2019).

https://www.georgiaencyclopedia.org/articles/government-politics/button-gwinnett-1735-1777/. Accessed June 30, 2023.

[2] J. C. Flanagan speculates that the Masons descend from George Mason, a signer of the Declaration of Independence, and Charles Mason, who participated in the survey of the Mason-Dixon Line in 1767. See *History of Gwinnett County Georgia, 1818–1960*, Gwinnett County Historical Society, 1959, 532.

[3] Bradley Rice, "Putting Gwinnett County in Historical Perspective," *Gwinnett County, Georgia, and the Transformation of the American South, 1818–2018*, eds. Michael Gagnon and Matthew Hild (Athens: University of Georgia Press, 2022), 1. Census records from 1820, 1830, 1840, 1850, and 1860 indicate that the family of G. F. Mason, from which Wayne and Jimmy Mason descend, was not included in the 133 plantation owners, nor did they own slaves.

[4] Elliott Brack, *Gwinnett: A Little above Atlanta* (Norcross, GA: Gwinnett Forum, 2012), 31.

[5] Rice, "Putting Gwinnett County in Historical Perspective," 1.

[6] Articles of Agreement and Cession Regarding Georgia's Western Lands, 1802, Georgia Archives. https://vault.georgiaarchives.org/ digital/collection/adhoc/id/420/. Accessed October 24, 2023.

[7] Richard A. Cook, "Cherokee and Creek Agency: Gwinnett County before the Button," in *Gwinnett County, Georgia, and the Transformation of the American South, 1818–2018*, eds. Michael Gagnon and Matthew Hild (Athens: University of Georgia Press, 2022), 19.

[8] Tyler Boulware, "Cherokee Indians," *New Georgia Encyclopedia*, last modified August 24, 2020. https://www.georgiaencyclopedia.org/articles/history-archaeology/cherokee-indians/. Accessed June 3, 2023.

[9] Michael Gagnon, "Slavery and Cotton in Antebellum Gwinnett," in *Gwinnett County, Georgia, and the Transformation of the American South, 1818–2018*, eds. Michael Gagnon and Matthew Hild (Athens: University of Georgia Press, 2022), 41.

[10] Ibid.

[11] Ibid.

[12] Rice, "Putting Gwinnett County in Historical Perspective," 1.

[13] Gagnon, "Slavery and Cotton in Antebellum Gwinnett," 40.

[14] Ibid.

[15] Ibid, 41.

[16] Ibid.

[17] Ibid.

[18] Bill Kirby, *Dynamic Gwinnett: Legacy, Life, and Vision* (Atlanta: Longstreet Press, 1993), 40.

[19] Gagnon, "Slavery and Cotton in Antebellum Gwinnett," 55.

[20] Keith Hebert, "Reluctant Confederates, Steadfast Unionists, and Rebellious Slaves: Secession and the Civil War in Gwinnett County, 1860–1865," in *Gwinnett County, Georgia, and the Transformation of the American South, 1818–2018,* eds. Michael Gagnon and Matthew Hild (Athens: University of Georgia Press, 2022), 60.

[21] Ibid., 61.

[22] Kirby, *Dynamic Gwinnett,* 43.

[23] Hebert, "Reluctant Confederates," 65.

[24] Ibid., 72.

[25] Kirby, *Dynamic Gwinnett,* 37.

[26] Ibid., 38.

[27] Michael Gagnon and Matthew Hild, "Reconstruction and Race in Gwinnett and Northeast Georgia," in *Gwinnett County, Georgia, and the Transformation of the American South, 1818–2018,* eds. Michael Gagnon and Matthew Hild (Athens: University of Georgia Press, 2022), 80–93.

[28] R. Scott Huffard Jr., "Gwinnett on the Air-Line: Railroads and Town Building in Gwinnett County," in *Gwinnett County, Georgia, and the Transformation of the American South, 1818–2018,* eds. Michael Gagnon and Matthew Hild (Athens: University of Georgia Press, 2022), 94.

[29] Ibid.

[30] Ibid., 98.

[31] "Gwinnett Historic Courthouse," at https://www.gwinnettcounty.com/static/about_gwinnett/gcb2017/ghchouse.html. Accessed October 8, 2023.

[32] David Mason, "Luck and Pluck: The Life of Buck Buchanan," in *Gwinnett County, Georgia, and the Transformation of the American*

*South, 1818–2018*, eds. Michael Gagnon and Matthew Hild (Athens: University of Georgia Press, 2022), 135.

[33] Kirby, *Dynamic Gwinnett*, 29–35.

[34] Brack, *Gwinnett*, 125–26.

[35] Mary Panettiere, "Gwinnett County," *New Georgia Encyclopedia*, last modified July 7, 2022. https://www.georgiaencyclopedia.org/articles/counties-cities-neighborhoods/gwinnett-county/. Accessed October 5, 2023.

Chapter 2: An Engine for Growth

[1] Bill Kirby, *Dynamic Gwinnett: Legacy, Life and Vision* (Atlanta: Longstreet Press, 1993), 3–4.

[2] Darren Grem, "Henry W. Grady," *New Georgia Encyclopedia*, last modified February 1, 2022. https://www.georgiaencyclopedia.org/articles/arts-culture/henry-w-grady-1850-1889/. Accessed July 26, 2022.

[3] Harold E. Davis, "Henry Grady, the *Atlanta Constitution*, and the Politics of Farming in the 1880s," *The Georgia Historical Quarterly* 71/4 (Winter 1987): 571–600.

[4] Mary Panettiere. "Gwinnett County." *New Georgia Encyclopedia*, last modified July 7, 2022. https://www.georgiaencyclopedia.org/articles/counties-cities-neighborhoods/gwinnett-county/. Accessed October 3, 2021.

[5] "Gwinnett History: The Quick and Easy Lowdown on the History of Gwinnett," *Gwinnett Magazine*, 36–37. https://gwinnettmagazine.com/gwinnett-history/. No date. Accessed July 26, 2022.

[6] Tyler Estep, "Flashback Photos: Buford Was Once Home to the Country's Most Prolific Tannery," *Atlanta Journal-Constitution*, September 28, 2016. https://www.ajc.com/news/local/flashback-photos-buford-was-once-home-the-country-most-prolific-tannery. Accessed July 26, 2022.

[7] James C. Flanigan, *History of Gwinnett County* (Atlanta: Tyler and Company, 1943). Quoted in Kirby, *Dynamic Gwinnett*, 11.

[8] William D. Bryan, "Sprawling Fields of Cotton: The Boom and Bust of Cotton Culture in Gwinnett," in *Gwinnett County, Georgia, and the Transformation of the American South, 1818–2018*, eds. Mi-

chael Gagnon and Matthew Hild (Athens: University of Georgia Press, 2022), 157.

[9] Wayne Mason and Keith Mason, interview by Catherine Lewis, May 14, 2021.

[10] Jared Meade, "Father of PR, Ivy Lee, Pioneered Tactics We Use Today," *PR News*, August 24, 2020. https://www.prnewsonline.com/ivy-lee-crisis-history/, Accessed July 9, 2002. For a more detailed account of his life, see Ray Eldon Hiebert, *Courtier to the Crowd: Ivy Lee and the Development of Public Relations in America* (New York: PR Museum Press, 2017).

[11] Wayne and Keith Mason, interview by Catherine Lewis, April 6, 2021.

[12] Wayne Mason, interview by Catherine Lewis, March 22, 2021.

[13] Hank Huckaby would go on to become a Georgia state representative and chancellor of the University System of Georgia. Marti Fullerton would go on to work in the lieutenant governor's office and the governor's office. Then, in 1998, Fullerton was appointed commissioner of the Georgia Department of Labor by Governor Zell Miller.

[14] Keith Mason, interview by Catherine Lewis, February 22, 2021.

[15] "Leaders & Legends: Wayne Mason," *Gwinnett Magazine* (March 2022): 26. https://gwinnettmagazine.com/leaders-legends-wayne-mason/. Accessed October 1, 2022.

[16] Ibid.

[17] Wayne Mason, interview by Catherine Lewis, April 6, 2021.

[18] Ibid., March 22, 2021.

[19] Elliott Brack, *Gwinnett: A Little above Atlanta* (Norcross, GA: Gwinnett Forum, 2012), 33.

[20] Kirby, *Dynamic Gwinnett*, 6–7.

[21] Brack, *Gwinnett*, 33.

[22] Ibid., 34.

[23] Ibid.

[24] Ann Mason, interview by Catherine Lewis, October 9, 2023.

[25] Keith Mason, interview by Catherine Lewis, March 10, 2021.

[26] Richard Tucker, interview by Catherine Lewis, July 27, 2023.

[27] Tracey Mason, interview by Catherine Lewis, October 7, 2023.

[28] Kirby, *Dynamic Gwinnett*, 4.

[29] Brack, *Gwinnett*, 133.

[30] Ibid., 131.

[31] Tracey Mason, interview by Catherine Lewis, October 7, 2023. See also Brack, *Gwinnett*.

[32] Curt Yeomans, "After 100 Years, Snellville Has Grown but Still Remains a 'Mercantile' Town," *Gwinnett Daily Post*, August 20, 2023.

[33] City of Snellville, at https://www.snellville.org/about-snellville/history. Accessed September 25, 2023.

[34] Brack, *Gwinnett*, 138.

[35] Deanna M. Gillespie, "'Revolutionize Life in the Chattahoochee River Valley': Buford Dam and the Development of Northeastern Georgia, 1950–1970," *The Georgia Historical Quarterly* 50 (Winter 2017): 409.

[36] Ibid., 412.

[37] Brack, *Gwinnett*, 139.

[38] Gillespie, *Buford Dam*, 413–14.

[39] Brack, *Gwinnett*, 139.

[40] Gillespie, *Buford Dam*, 405.

[41] Ibid., 406.

[42] Ibid., 407.

[43] Brack, *Gwinnett*, 139.

[44] Ibid.

[45] Gillespie, *Buford Dam*, 421.

[46] Kathryn Nikolich, "Gwinnett County, Georgia, A Sunbelt Community: The Invention of a Postwar Suburb," Master's thesis, Georgia State University, January 16, 2015, 11.

[47] Roy Alexander, "Men in Despair," *Time*, August 13, 1956. Quoted in Brack, *Gwinnett*, 159.

[48] Ibid.

[49] Eugene Patterson, "Griffin Calls for Full Probe of Rock Quarry Prison," *Atlanta Constitution*, August 7, 1957; "Gwinnett Jury Praises Buford Prison Operation," *Atlanta Constitution*, September 18, 1957.

[50] Wayne Mason, interview by Catherine Lewis, May 14, 2021.

[51] Achsah Posey, "Cole Guilty on 2 Counts Out of 7," *Atlanta Constitution*, February 5, 1963.

[52] Nikolich, *Gwinnett County*, 26.

[53] "Syndicate-Style Crime Rings Blamed for Rising Car Thefts," *Atlanta Constitution*, April 18, 1964.

[54] ABC News, "Man Who Buried Girl Alive Becomes Doctor," November 5, 2002. https://abcnews.go.com/US/story?id=91055&page=1. Accessed September 3, 2023.

[55] "Larry Flynt, Lawyer 'Critical' After Lawrenceville Shooting," *Atlanta Constitution*, March 7, 1978, 1.

[56] Nikolich, *Gwinnett County*, 14.

Chapter 3: Laying the Groundwork

[1] Elliott E. Brack, *Gwinnett: A Little above Atlanta* (Norcross: Gwinnett Forum, 2012) 171.

[2] Ibid.

[3] Edward Hatfield, "Of Malls and MARTA: Gwinnett in the Late Twentieth Century," in *Gwinnett County, Georgia, and the Transformation of the American South, 1818–2018*, eds. Michael Gagnon and Matthew Hild (Athens: University of Georgia Press, 2022) 209.

[4] Ibid., 209.

[5] Brack, *Gwinnett*, 202.

[6] Ibid., 203.

[7] Wayne Mason, interview by Catherine Lewis, September 14, 2023.

[8] Wayne Kelley, "Buford Quarry Changes Duo," *Atlanta Journal and Constitution*, December 12, 1965.

[9] Joe Crespino, *In Search of Another Country: Mississippi and the Conservative Counterrevolution* (Princeton, NJ: Princeton University Press, 2007). For more information, see chapter 6.

[10] Quoted in Kathryn Nikolich, "Gwinnett County, Georgia, A Sunbelt Community: The Invention of a Postwar Suburb," Master's thesis, Georgia State University, January 16, 2015. See also "Republican Party Platform of 1968," August 5, 1968, *The American Presidency Project*. https://www.presidency.ucsb.edu/documents/republican-party-platform-1968. Accessed September 3, 2023.

[11] Brack, *Gwinnett*, 205.

[12] Ibid., 169.

[13] Ibid., 170.

[14] Ibid., 207.

[15] The American Presidency Project, "Annual Message to Congress on the State of the Union," January 5, 1956. https://www.presidency.ucsb.edu/documents/annual-message-the-congress-the-state-the-union-11. Accessed September 3, 2023.

[16] Nikolich, *Gwinnett County*, 20.

[17] Ibid.

[18] Hatfield, "Gwinnett in the Late Twentieth Century," 209.

[19] William E. Schmidt, "Once-Rural Georgia County Now Has the Fastest Growth in the U.S.," *New York Times*, June 2, 1985.

[20] Quoted in Hatfield, "Gwinnett in the Late Twentieth Century," 210.

[21] Wayne Mason interview by Catherine Lewis, February 22, 2022.

[22] Brack, *Gwinnett*, 34.

[23] Wayne Mason, interview by Catherine Lewis, February 22, 2022.

[24] Brack, *Gwinnett*, 34.

[25] Ibid., 35.

[26] Wayne Mason, interview by Catherine Lewis, February 22, 2022.

[27] Richard Tucker, interview by Catherine Lewis, July 27, 2023.

[28] US Census, "Standard Metropolitan Statistical Area (SMSAs) and Components, 1960," http://www.census.gov/population/metro/files/lists/historical/60mfips.txt. Accessed September 3, 2023.

[29] Emmie Martin, "Here's How Much Housing Prices Have Skyrocketed Over the Last 50 Years," *CNBC*, June 23, 2017. https://www.cnbc.com/2017/06/23/how-much-housing-prices-have-risen-since-1940.html. Accessed July 27, 2022.

[30] Brack, *Gwinnett*, 35.

[31] Ibid.

[32] Richard Tucker, interview by Catherine Lewis, July 27, 2023.

[33] Wayne Mason, interview by Catherine Lewis, September 14, 2023.

[34] "Leaders & Legends: Wayne Mason," *Gwinnett Magazine* (March 2022). https://gwinnettmagazine.com/leaders-legends-wayne-mason/. Accessed October 1, 2022. 26–27.

[35] Richard Tucker, interview by Catherine Lewis, July 27, 2023.

[36] Ibid.

Chapter 4: Servant Leadership

[1] "Leaders & Legends: Wayne Mason," *Gwinnett Magazine* (March 2022): 27. https://gwinnettmagazine.com/leaders-legends-wayne-mason/. Accessed October 1, 2022.

[2] Peter Kent, "Obituary, Jimmy Mason, 61, Former Legislator," *Atlanta Journal*, June 6, 1998, 36.

[3] Elliott Brack, *Gwinnett: A Little above Atlanta* (Norcross, GA: Gwinnett Forum, 2012), 37.

[4] Ibid.

[5] Kent, "Obituary, Jimmy Mason," 36.

[6] Richard Tucker, interview by Catherine Lewis, July 27, 2023. Jimmy displayed a plaque on his desk that read "There is no limit to what a man can do if he doesn't care who gets the credit." When Jimmy died, Wayne moved the plaque to his desk as a reminder. Tracey Mason, interview by Catherine Lewis, October 7, 2023.

[7] Sam Williams, interview by Catherine Lewis, August 22, 2023.

[8] Wayne Mason, interview by Catherine Lewis, September 14, 2023.

[9] Tracey Mason, interview by Catherine Lewis, October 22, 2023.

[10] Georgia Ports Authority, "Growing Big–Mason Mega Rail," https://gaports.com/blog/growing-big-mason-mega-rail/. Accessed September 23, 2023.

[11] Brack, *Gwinnett*, 37.

[12] Ibid.

[13] Ibid., 265.

[14] Ibid., 266.

[15] Bill Buchanan, "Poker Rob Suspect Arrested," *Atlanta Journal*, August 15, 1972, 8.

[16] Kent, "Obituary, Jimmy Mason," 36.

[17] Wayne Mason, interview by Catherine Lewis, February 22, 2022.

[18] Brack, *Gwinnett*, 37–38.

[19] Wayne Mason, interview by Catherine Lewis, September 14, 2023.

[20] Wayne Shackleford, interview by Clifford Kuhn, 2007. Georgia State University: Georgia Documentation Project (June 18, 2007). Quoted in Kathryn Nikolich, "Gwinnett County, Georgia, A Sunbelt Community: The Invention of a Postwar Suburb," Master's thesis, Georgia State University, January 16, 2015, 41.

[21] Sam Williams, interview by Catherine Lewis, August 22, 2023.

[22] Wayne Mason, interview by Catherine Lewis, September 14, 2023.

[23] Gwinnett.com, at https://www.gwinnettcounty.com/web/gwinnett/aboutgwinnett/history. Accessed May 21, 2023.

[24] "Wayne Mason," *Gwinnett Magazine*, 27.

[25] "Tracey Mason: Delivering on a Legacy of Compassion and Commitment to Gwinnett," *Gwinnett Magazine*. https://gwinnettmagazine.com/tracey-mason-delivering-on-a-legacy-of-compassion-and-commitment-to-gwinnett/. Accessed September 15, 2023.

[26] Wayne Mason, interview by Catherine Lewis, February 22, 2022.

[27] Curt Yeomans, "Former Gwinnett Chairman Wayne Mason's Contributions to County's Water System Highlighted with Plaque and Sculpture," *Gwinnett Daily Post*, December 11, 2022. https://www.gwinnettdailypost.com/local/former-gwinnett-chairman-wayne-masons-contributions-to-countys-water-system-highlighted-with-plaque-sculpture/article_a55ae4fe-3c16-11eb-bb69-6b9a73516f07.html. Accessed May 23, 2022.

[28] Jim Henderson, interview by Catherine Lewis, October 11, 2023.

[29] "Wayne Mason," *Gwinnett Magazine*.

[30] Ibid.

[31] Brack, *Gwinnett*, 256–57.

[32] Ibid.

[33] Wayne Mason, interview by Catherine Lewis, September 14, 2023.

[34] Quoted in Brack, *Gwinnett*, 262.

[35] Ibid., 262–63.

[36] Nikolich, *Gwinnett County*, 42.

[37] Brack, *Gwinnett*, 207.

[38] Nikolich, *Gwinnett County*, 42.

[39] Walter Hellerstein, "Michelin Tire Corp *v.* Wages: Enhanced State Power to Tax Imports," *The Supreme Court Review*, 1976: 106–107. Quoted in Nikolich, *Gwinnett County*, 430.

[40] Bill MacNabb, "Gwinnett Turns Down Housing," *Atlanta Constitution*, May 24, 1972, 8A.

[41] Wayne Mason, interview by Catherine Lewis, October 24, 2023.

[42] Nikolich, *Gwinnett County*, 61.

[43] Mark Berman, "City Schools Lose 5,000," *Atlanta Constitution*, August 23, 1974, 10A.

[44] Emma Edmonds and Jerry Schwartz, "Gwinnett Dares to Tackle New Schooling Ideas," *Atlanta Constitution*, April 24, 1979.

[45] Gwinnett County Schools Office of Research and Evaluation, at https://www.gcpsk12.org/domain/12334. Accessed October 1, 2022.

[46] Wayne Mason, interview by Catherine Lewis, September 14, 2023.

[47] Alia Pharr, "Gwinnett School Board Ends Superintendent Wilbanks' Contract Early," *Atlanta Journal-Constitution*, March 19, 2021. https://www.ajc.com/news/gwinnett-school-board-ends-superintendents-wilbanks-contract-early/FGJNBMTNOZDN7C5AQUFYM7O52Y. Accessed April 4, 2024.

[48] Alia Malik, "Wilbanks' Era Ends after 25 Years Leading Gwinnett School District," *Atlanta Journal-Constitution*, July 30, 2021. https://www.ajc.com/news/atlanta-news/wilbanks-era-ends-after-25-years-leading-gwinnett-school-district/LDYGPKIXHZBXHPCZ2KGFEPREDI/. Accessed September 23, 2023.

[49] "Wayne Mason," *Gwinnett Magazine*, 27.

[50] Ibid.

[51] Ibid.

[52] Yeomans, "Wayne Mason's Contributions." https://www.gwinnettdailypost.com/local/former-gwinnett-chairman-wayne-masons-contributions-to-countys-water-system-highlighted-with-plaque-sculpture/article_a55ae4fe-3c16-11eb-bb69-6b9a73516f07.html. Accessed October 2, 2023.

[53] Wayne Shackelford interview by Clifford Kuhn, quoted in Nikolich, *Gwinnett County*, 43.

Chapter 5: A Rocky Road

[1] Edward Hatfield, "Of Malls and MARTA: Gwinnett in the Late Twentieth Century," in *Gwinnett County, Georgia, and the Transformation of the American South, 1818–2018* (Athens: University of Georgia Press, 2022), eds. Michael Gagnon and Matthew Hild, 206–207.

[2] Ibid., 207.

[3] Ibid.

[4] Ibid., 214.

[5] Ibid.

[6] Ibid., 212.

[7] Ibid.

[8] Ibid., 213. See also Tom Teepen, "Paying a MARTA Penny Can be a Boon," *Atlanta Constitution*, July 26, 1990, and Douglas Lavin, "Gwinnett Voters are Likely to Decide MARTA Growth," *Atlanta Constitution*, June 6, 1990.

[9] Wayne Mason, interview by Catherine Lewis, September 14, 2023.

[10] Tyler Estep, "In Deeply Diverse Gwinnett, White Residents Confront Minority Status," *Atlanta Journal-Constitution*, November 24, 2017. https://www.ajc.com/news/local-govt--politics/deeply-diverse-gwinnett-white-residents-confront-minority-status/BQXjuWUwGW0tMQNyf4hQTO/. Accessed May 22, 2023.

[11] Wayne Mason, interview by Catherine Lewis, August 14, 2023.

[12] Elliott Brack, *Gwinnett: A Little above Atlanta* (Norcross, GA: Gwinnett Forum, 2012), 277.

[13] Ibid., 284–86.

[14] Ibid., 289.

[15] Wayne Mason, interview by Catherine Lewis, August 14, 2023.

[16] Brack, *Gwinnett*, 36–37.

[17] Ibid., 40.

[18] Ibid., 41, and "Obituary, Jimmy Mason, 61, Former Legislator," *Atlanta Journal*, June 6, 1998, 36.

[19] Brack, *Gwinnett*, 41.

[20] City of Snellville, "Snellville History," at https://www.snellville.org/about-snellville/history. Accessed September 10, 2023.

[21] Brack, *Gwinnett*, 36.

[22] Scott Horsley, "Think Inflation Is Bad Now? Let's Take a Step Back to the 1970s," NPR, *Weekend Edition*, May 29, 2021. https://www.npr.org/2021/05/29/1001023637/think-inflation-is-bad-now-lets-take-a-step-back-to-the-1970s. Accessed October 15, 2023.

[23] Michael Urquhart and Marillyn A. Hewson, "Unemployment Continued to Rise in 1982 as Recession Deepened," *Bureau of Labor Statistics Monthly Labor Review*, February 1983.

[24] Brack, *Gwinnett*, 36–37.

[25] Ibid., 333.

[26] Ibid., 336.

[27] Ibid., 337.

[28] Wayne Mason, interview by Catherine Lewis, September 14, 2023.

[29] Brack, *Gwinnett*, 42.

[30] Ibid., 42–46.

[31] Ibid.

[32] Richard Tucker, interview by Catherine Lewis, July 27, 2023.

[33] Bartow Morgan, interview by Catherine Lewis, August 31, 2023.

[34] Wayne Mason, interview by Catherine Lewis, September 14, 2023.

Chapter 6: A New Era: From Braselton to the Beltline

[1] Bill Kirby, *Dynamic Gwinnett: Legacy, Life, and Vision* (Atlanta: Longstreet Press, 1993), 3.

[2] Ibid.

[3] Ibid.

[4] Elliott Brack, *Gwinnett: A Little above Atlanta* (Norcross, GA: Gwinnett Forum, 2012), 47.

[5] Bill Osinski, "The Town That Kim Forgot," *Chicago Tribune*, May 12, 1992. https://www.chicagotribune.com/news/ct-xpm-1992-03-12-9201230528-story.html. Accessed May 21, 2023.

[6] Brack, *Gwinnett*, 46.

[7] Wayne Mason, interview by Catherine Lewis, September 9, 2023.

[8] Brack, *Gwinnett*, 46.

[9] Ibid., 46.

[10] Ben Smith, "King of the Deal," *Atlanta Constitution*, November 13, 2005, A1, A10.

[11] Ibid., A10.

[12] Ibid.

[13] Ibid.

[14] Ibid.

[15] Ibid.

[16] Ibid.

[17] Scott Mall, "FreightWaves Classics: Port of Savannah Has Experienced Tremendous Growth," *FreightWaves,* March 16, 2021. https://www.freightwaves.com/news/freightwaves-classics-port-of-savannah-has-experienced-tremendous-growth. Accessed September 24, 2023.

[18] Ibid.

[19] Mary Ann DeMuth, "Georgia Ports' 75 Years of Success," *Georgia Trend* (October 31, 2020). https://www.georgiatrend.com/2020/10/31/75-years-of-success/. Accessed September 24, 2023.

[20] Keith Mason, interview by Catherine Lewis, October 6, 2023.

[21] Ethan Davidson, "The Atlanta BeltLine: A Green Future," *Public Roads* (December 2, 2011). https://beltline.org/2011/12/02/ history-of-atlanta-beltline-project-in-public-roads-magazine/. Accessed November 28, 2022.

[22] Bill Torpy, "The Beltline Guy, 20 Years After a Darn Good Term Paper," *Atlanta Journal-Constitution*, December 9, 2019. https://www.ajc.com/news/local/torpy-large-the-beltline-guy-years-after-darn-good-term-paper/pcrMCbz69etezThihCVGjN/. Accessed April 24, 2023.

[23] Sam Williams, interview by Catherine Lewis, August 22, 2023.

[24] PATH Foundation, at https://www.pathfoundation.org/. Accessed October 1, 2023.

[25] Torpy, "Beltline Guy," Accessed April 24, 2023.

[26] Wayne Mason, interview by Catherine Lewis, September 14, 2023.

[27] Mara Shalhoup, "Gwinnett Mega-Developer Mason Sells Beltline Land," *Creative Loafing* (April 19, 2007). https://creativeloafing.com/content-206003-gwinnett-mega-developer-mason-sells-his-beltline. Accessed November 28, 2022.

[28] Thomas Wheatley, "Critics Question Beltline Officials about Land Deal," *Creative Loafing*, December 17, 2008. https://creativeloafing.com/content-170517-critics-question-beltline-officials-about-land. Accessed November 28, 2022.

[29] Ibid.

[30] "How Long Did the Great Recession Last?" *Forbes* (October 19, 2022). https://www.forbes.com/sites/qai/2022/10/19/how-long-did-the-great-recession-last-in-2008/?sh=4e07809456b0. Accessed November 28, 2022.

[31] Hattie Dorsey, interview by Catherine Lewis, July 20, 2023.

[32] Sam Williams, interview by Catherine Lewis, September 22, 2023.

[33] "Leaders & Legends: Wayne Mason," *Gwinnett Magazine* (March 2022): 29. https://gwinnettmagazine.com/leaders-legends-wayne-mason/. Accessed October 1, 2022.

[34] Dan Chapman, "Hard Times for Gwinnett's Master of the Deal," *Atlanta Journal-Constitution*, January 5, 2010. https://www.ajc.com/business/hard-times-for-gwinnett-master-the-deal/akxV24X2yo0BFocYIWszEL/. Accessed November 22, 2022.

[35] Ibid.

[36] J. Scott Trubey, "Family of Atlanta Developer Wayne Mason Sued for $137M," *Atlanta Business Chronicle*, July 20, 2015. https://www.bizjournals.com/atlanta/news/2015/07/20/family-of-atlanta-developer-wayne-mason-sued-for.html. Accessed November 27, 2022.

[37] Ibid.

[38] Brack quoted in Chapman, "Hard Times."

Chapter 7: Giving Back and Passing the Torch

[1] Elliott Brack, *Gwinnett: A Little above Atlanta* (Norcross, GA: Gwinnett Forum, 2012), 367.

[2] Atlanta Regional Commission, "Cultural Assessment of the Atlanta Region," May 2023. https://cdn.atlantaregional.org/wp-content/uploads/cultural-assessment-2023.pdf. Accessed October 19, 2023.

[3] Brack, *Gwinnett*, 370–71.

[4] "Scientific-Atlanta Has a History of Philanthropy," *Gwinnett Daily Post*, November 18, 2005. https://www.gwinnettdailypost.com/archive/scientific-atlanta-has-history-of-philanthropy/article_51c31db3-9a3e-53a8-8d2b-1b8b673b0946.html. Accessed October 19, 2023.

[5] "Clyde and Sandra Strickland Named Public Library Champions," *Gwinnett Magazine*, January 24, 2023. https://gwinnettmagazine.com/clyde-and-sandra-strickland-named-public-library-champions/. Accessed October 19, 2023.

[6] Brack, *Gwinnett*, 47.

[7] Ibid.

[8] "Leaders and Legends: Wayne Mason," *Gwinnett Magazine*, 29. https://gwinnettmagazine.com/leaders-legends-wayne-mason/. Accessed September 7, 2023.

[9] Ibid.

[10] Brack, *Gwinnett*, 506.

[11] Ibid., 365.

[12] Ibid.

[13] Atlanta Community Food Bank, "About Us," at https://www.acfb.org/history/#:~:text=over%2040%20years,children%20and%20seniors%20in%20need. Accessed September 9, 2023.

[14] "Wayne Mason," *Gwinnett Magazine*, 29. https://gwinnett magazine.com/leaders-legends-wayne-mason/. Accessed October 1, 2022.

[15] Brack, *Gwinnett*, 303–304.

[16] Ibid., 48.

[17] Ibid., 498.

[18] Bartow Morgan Jr., interview with Catherine Lewis, August 31, 2023.

[19] Georgia Gwinnett College, "Early History," at https://www .ggc.edu/about-ggc/ggc-at-a-glance/ggc-at-a-glance-history#:~:text= GGC%20opened%20its%20doors%20to,in%20more%20than%20100%2 0years. Accessed September 7, 2023.

[20] "Acts and Resolutions of the General Assembly of the State of Georgia," at http://mydocs.dot.ga.gov/info/honorariums/Resolutions/ 2019_WayneMasonHighway.pdf. Accessed April 1, 2023.

[21] Curt Yeomans, "Former Gwinnett Chairman Wayne Mason's Contributions to County's Water System Highlighted with Plaque and Sculpture," *Gwinnett Daily Post*, December 11, 2022. https://www.gwinnettdailypost.com/local/former-gwinnett-chairman-wayne-masons-contributions-to-countys-water-system-highlighted-with-plaque-sculpture/article_a55ae4fe-3c16-11eb-bb69-6b9a73516f07.html. Accessed May 23, 2022.

[22] Ibid.

[23] Keith Mason, interview by Catherine Lewis, October 25, 2023.

[24] Ibid.

[25] Ibid. See also University of Georgia, "Keith Mason Papers," at https://sclfind.libs.uga.edu/sclfind/view?docId=ead/RBRL250KM.xml . Accessed September 7, 2023.

[26] Bob Short, interview by Keith Mason, November 18, 2008. Richard B. Russell Library for Political Research and Studies, University of Georgia. https://ohms.libs.uga.edu/viewer.php?cachefile=russell/ RBRL220ROGP-057.xml. Accessed October 25, 2023.

[27] Keith Mason, interview by Catherine Lewis, October 25, 2023.

[28] Ibid.

[29] Bob Short interview by Keith Mason, November 18, 2008. Richard B. Russell Library for Political Research and Studies, Universi-

ty of Georgia. https://ohms.libs.uga.edu/viewer.php?cachefile=russell/RBRL220ROGP-057.xml. Accessed October 25, 2023.

[30] Keith Mason, interview by Catherine Lewis, October 25, 2023.

[31] Ibid.

[32] "Tracey Mason: Delivering on a Legacy of Compassion and Commitment to Gwinnett," *Gwinnett Magazine*. https://gwinnettmagazine.com/tracey-mason-delivering-on-a-legacy-of-compassion-and-commitment-to-gwinnett/. Accessed September 15, 2023.

[33] Ibid.

[34] Tracey Mason, interview by Catherine Lewis, October 7, 2023.

[35] Ibid.

[36] Ibid.

[37] Ibid.

[38] Ibid.

[39] Ibid.

[40] Keith Mason, interview by Catherine Lewis, March 10, 2021.

Chapter 8: Dynamic and Diverse

[1] Elliott Brack, *Gwinnett: A Little above Atlanta* (Norcross, GA: Gwinnett Forum, 2012), 48.

[2] Bill Kirby, *Dynamic Gwinnett: Legacy, Life, and Vision* (Atlanta: Longstreet Press, 1993), 13.

[3] Becky Little, "How the 'Party of Lincoln,' Won Over the Once Democratic South," April 10, 2019, History.com. https://www.history.com/news/how-the-party-of-lincoln-won-over-the-once-democratic-south. Accessed November 28, 2022.

[4] Ibid.

[5] James Cobb, "Why a Key Georgia County Flipped from Red to Blue—And What It Means for Democrats," *Fortune* (December 27, 2020). https://fortune.com/2020/12/27/georgia-election-2020-gwinnett-county-flipped/. Accessed November 28, 2022.

[6] Kirby, *Dynamic Gwinnett*, 13.

[7] Cobb, "Key Georgia County Flipped."

[8] Ibid.

[9] Ibid.

[10] Marko Maunula, "From Burbs to Pueblo: Mass Immigration and Gwinnett County's Demographic Revolution, 1990–2020," in *Gwinnett County Georgia and the Transformation of the American South, 1818–2018*, eds. Michael Gagnon and Matthew Hild (Athens: University of Georgia Press, 2022), 235.

[11] Ibid., 226.

[12] Ibid.

[13] Ibid., 227. See Migration Policy Institute at https://www. migrationpolicy.org/data/state-profiles/state/demographics/GA. Accessed May 21, 2023.

[14] Haisten Willis, "Gwinnett County: Dynamic and Diverse," *Georgia Trend* (August 31, 2020). https://www.georgiatrend.com/2020/08/31/gwinnett-county-dynamic-and-diverse/. Accessed May 22, 2023.

[15] Ibid.

[16] Matt Vasilogambros, "The Most Diverse County in the Southeast Is Run Almost Entirely by White Politicians," *Atlantic* (April 2, 2015). https://www.theatlantic.com/politics/archive/2015/04/the-most-diverse-county-in-the-southeast-is-run-almost-entirely-by-white-politicians/431922/. Accessed October 9, 2023.

[17] Yelp, s.v. "Santa Fe Mall," Madelyn A., review, https://www.yelp.com/biz/santa-fe-mall-duluth?adjust_creative=togo&hrid=6DaXRRhok2QzB7zUOV8UDQ&utm_campaign=yelp_feed&utm_medium=feed_v2&utm_source=togo. Accessed October 9, 2023.

[18] Tyler Estep, "In Deeply Diverse Gwinnett, White Residents Confront Minority Status," *Atlanta Journal-Constitution*, November 24, 2017. https://www.ajc.com/news/local-govt--politics/deeply-diverse-gwinnett-white-residents-confront-minority-status/BQXjuWUwGW0tMQNyf4hQTO/. Accessed May 22, 2023.

[19] Maunula, "Demographic Revolution," 230.

[20] Ibid., 231–32.

[21] Ibid., 232.

[22] Vasilogambros, "Most Diverse County."

https://www.theatlantic.com/politics/archive/2015/04/the-most-diverse-county-in-the-southeast-is-run-almost-entirely-by-white-politicians/431922/. Accessed May 21, 2023.

[23] Georgia House of Representatives, "Pedro 'Pete' Marin," https://www.house.ga.gov/Representatives/en-US/member.aspx?Member=163&Member=163/. Accessed May 22, 2023.

[24] Tyler Estep, "Expansion of Long-Debated Lilburn Mosque to Take 'A Few Years,'" *Gwinnett Daily Post*, November 21, 2011. https://www.gwinnettdailypost.com/archive/expansion-of-long-debated-lilburn-mosque-to-take-a-few-years/article_4fab3805-155d-53d8-8a9d-f15bc2beea1a.html. Accessed May 22, 2023. Shane Blatt, "Lilburn Mosque Foes Allege Harassment," *Atlanta Journal-Constitution*, June 18, 2010. https://www.ajc.com/news/local/lilburn-mosque-foes-allege-harassment/1P9vpSaROJRrI1JcSd3JbI/. Accessed May 22, 2023.

[25] Joel Anderson, "Mosque Dispute Divides Lilburn," *Atlanta Journal-Constitution*, October 5, 2011. https://www.ajc.com/news/local/mosque-dispute-divides-lilburn/LvPOrdHdYiGajVPKkkaL8M/. Accessed May 22, 2023.

[26] Ibid.

[27] Estep, "White Residents Confront Minority Status."

[28] Pew Research Center, "Controversies Over Mosques and Islamic Centers Across the U.S.," September 27, 2012. https://assets.pewresearch.org/wp-content/uploads/sites/11/2012/09/2012Mosque-Map.pdf. Accessed October 9, 2023.

[29] Estep, "White Residents Confront Minority Status."

[30] Sam Gringlas, "In Gwinnett, Local Redistricting Spurs Debate about Demographic and Political Change," WABE, March 1, 2022. https://www.wabe.org/in-gwinnett-county-local-redistricting-spurs-debates-about-demographic-and-political-change/

[31] Mark Niesse and Maya T. Prabhu, "Georgia Redistricting Signed into Law and Lawsuits Quickly Follow," *Atlanta Journal-Constitution*, December 1, 2021.

[32] Brack, *Gwinnett*, 48.

[33] "Tracey Mason: Delivering on a Legacy of Compassion and Commitment to Gwinnett," *Gwinnett Magazine*. https://gwinnettmagazine.com/tracey-mason-delivering-on-a-legacy-of-compassion-and-commitment-to-gwinnett/

Epilogue: The World According to Wayne

[1] Wayne Mason, interview by Catherine Lewis, September 15, 2022.

[2] Wayne Mason, interview by Catherine Lewis, October 20, 2023.

[3] Ben Smith, "King of the Deal," *Atlanta Constitution*, November 13, 2005, A1, A10.

[4] Megan DeMatteo, "The Average American Has $90,460 in Debt—Here's How Much Debt Americans Have at Every Age," *CNBC*, November 18, 2021. https://www.cnbc.com/select/average-american-debt-by-age/. Accessed September 30, 2022.

[5] Nationwide, Inc., at https://www.nationwide.com/lc/resources/personal-finance/articles/living-within-your-means. Accessed October 2, 2022.

[6] Capital One, "7 Tips to Help You Live Within or Below Your Means," March 13, 2023, https://www.capitalone.com/learn-grow/money-management/live-below-your-means/. Accessed September 7, 2023.

[7] Smith, "King of the Deal," A1, A10.

[8] Dan Cable, "What You Should Follow Instead of Your Passion," *Harvard Business Review* (November 24, 2020). https://hbr.org/2020/11/what-you-should-follow-instead-of-your-passion. Accessed October 22, 2023.

[9] Ibid.

[10] Lauren Howe, John Jachimowicz, and Jochen Menges, "Your Job Doesn't Have to be Your Passion," *Harvard Business Review* (June 4, 2021). https://hbr.org/2021/06/your-job-doesnt-have-to-be-your-passion, Accessed October 22, 2023.

[11] Ibid.

[12] Wayne Mason, interview by Catherine Lewis, September 14, 2023.

[13] Lisa Song Sutton, "How to Diversify Your Business Interests," *Entrepreneur*, July 5, 2022. https://www.entrepreneur.com/starting-a-business/why-you-need-to-diversify-your-business-interests-and-how/428870. Accessed October 22, 2023.

[14] Wayne Mason, interview by Catherine Lewis, September 14, 2023.

[15] Rick Barvin, "Leadership with Purpose and Building a Giving Culture," *Forbes* (December 6, 2022). https://www.forbes.com/sites/forbesbusinesscouncil/2022/12/06/leadership-with-purpose-and-building-a-giving-culture/#:~:text=In%20addition%20to%20boosting%20overall,to%20lead%20a%20volunteer%20day. Accessed October 22, 2023.

[16] Cleveland Clinic, "Why Giving Is Good for Your Health," December 7, 2022. https://health.clevelandclinic.org/why-giving-is-good-for-your-health/#:~:text=As%20you%20help%20someone%20or,sense%20of%20connection%20with%20others). Accessed October 22, 2023.

[17] Ibid.

[18] Wayne Mason, interview by Catherine Lewis, September 14, 2023.

[19] Ibid.

[20] Tina Hovsepian, "Business and People: Why Relationships Are Essential for a Successful Business," *Forbes* (July 20, 2018). https://www.forbes.com/sites/forbeslacouncil/2018/07/20/business-and-people-why-relationships-are-essential-for-a-successful-business/?sh=142ece1974f2. Accessed October 22, 2023.

[21] Ibid.

[22] Wayne Mason, interview by Catherine Lewis, September 14, 2023.

[23] "Leaders & Legends: Wayne Mason," *Gwinnett Magazine* (March 2022): 28. https://gwinnettmagazine.com/leaders-legends-wayne-mason/. Accessed October 1, 2022.

[24] Wayne Mason, interview by Catherine Lewis, September 14, 2023.

[25] Rebecca Knight, "How to Stop Micromanaging Your Team," *Harvard Business Review* (August 21, 2015). https://hbr.org/2015/08/how-to-stop-micromanaging-your-team?registration=success. Accessed October 22, 2023.

[26] See Amy Jen Su and Muriel Maignan Wilkins, *Own the Room: Discover Your Signature Voice to Master Your Leadership Presence* (Boston: Harvard Business Review Press, 2013).

[27] Paul Jones and Michael Best, "Two Cheers for Cheerleading," *Milwaukee Journal Sentinel*, April 17, 2016. https://www.jsonline.com/story/money/business/onramp/blog/2016/04/18/two-cheers-for-cheerleading/84885628/. Accessed October 13, 2023.

[28] Wayne Mason, interview by Catherine Lewis, September 14, 2023.

[29] Ibid.

[30] Justin Grome, "The Importance of Taking Risks in Business," *Forbes* (December 2, 2021). https://www.forbes.com/sites/forbes businesscouncil/2021/12/02/the-importance-of-taking-risks-in-business/?sh=1affb642555d. Accessed October 1, 2023.

[31] Ulrik Juul Christensen, "Why Character May be the Secret Ingredient for Future Success," *Forbes* (May 11, 2022). https://www.forbes.com/sites/ulrikjuulchristensen/2022/05/11/why-character-may-be-the-secret-ingredient-for-future-success/?sh=10c60553538f. Accessed October 3, 2023.

[32] Tracey Mason, interview by Catherine Lewis, October 7, 2023.

[33] Ann Mason, interview by Catherine Lewis, October 9, 2023.

[34] Jim Henderson, interview by Catherine Lewis, October 11, 2023.

[35] "Wayne Mason," *Gwinnett Magazine*, 29. https://gwinnettmagazine.com/leaders-legends-wayne-mason/. Accessed October 1, 2022.

# Acknowledgments

This book, like all such projects, involved the assistance, hard work, and support of numerous people. I would like to begin by thanking the Mason family, especially Wayne and Ann Mason, Keith Mason, Tracey Mason, Tina Mason Carico, Teresa Mason Waters, Kay Hamil, Kristy English, and Kim Hanna. Shelly Kaczynski was particularly helpful in all aspects of the book, from scheduling interviews, to helping identify photographs, to editing the manuscript. Her assistance was invaluable. I am especially grateful to Senator Sam Nunn and Governor Roy Barnes for contributing the foreword and preface. They both have extraordinary stories and major contributions to public service, and it was a pleasure working with them both. Valeria MacPhail and Sharon Holt in their respective offices warrant a special thanks. Steve Wrigley, the former chancellor of the University System of Georgia, was the first person to bring Wayne's story to my attention, and I am grateful to him for his foresight.

There are a number of journalists and historians who have written widely about Gwinnett, including Elliott Brack, James C. Flanagan, and Bill Kirby. All good scholarship draws upon those who came before, and I am especially grateful for their work. The historians who contributed to in *Gwinnett County, Georgia, and the Transformation of the American South, 1818-2018*, edited by Michael Gagnon and Matthew Hild and published by the University of Georgia Press in 2022, was an especially helpful resource.

I am thankful to the people who agreed to be interviewed for this book, including Sam Williams, Hattie Dorsey, Richard Tucker, Jim Henderson, and Bartow Morgan Jr. A special thanks to Melna Henderson, Jim Henderson, Steve Wrigley for also agreeing to read a draft. A special thanks to Dr. Jennifer Dickey, my longtime friend and colleague at Kennesaw State University. While working on this project, she was writing a book with University of Georgia Press about the state's historic sites. We spent a great deal of time reading each other's manuscripts, and her keen and critical eye made this a better book. The team at Mercer University Press—Marc Jolley, Marsha Luttrell, Mary Beth Kosowski, Jenny Toole, Kelley Land—has been dedicated partners from the beginning, and I am so grateful for their patience with and commitment to the project.

In addition to those already mentioned, I also want to acknowledge a number of people who have contributed so much to Gwinnett County over the years and helped the Mason family do their good work: Zell and Shirley Miller, Scott Hudgens and his family, Thomas Wheeler, Steven Gaultney, Virgil Williams and his family and colleagues, Doug Wilkerson, Roddy Sturdivant, Tim Connolly, Doug McCurdy, A.M. "Buddy" Redd, E.R. Snell Construction Company and family, David and Robin Snell, John D. Stephens, Rudy and Millard Bowen, the lawyers and staff at Webb, Tanner, Powell, Martz & Wilson, the lawyers and staff at Andersen, Tate & Carr, Gerald Davidson, Homer Stark, Jim Henderson, John Mobley, Ted Hester, the Council for Quality Growth and its many leaders (including its founding chair Ray Weeks and executive directors Helen Tapp and Michael Paris), Alvin Wilbanks, Alton Crews, J.W. Benefield, colleagues on the Gwinnett Commission (including Bill Atkinson, Ray Gunnin, Julian Archer, Guy Stokes, K. C. Bowen, Edwin Howard, and Maron Buice), Tom Moreland, Emmett Clower, Jim Pack, Bartow Morgan III and his sons, Leo Rainey, Steve Williams, Glenn White, Steve Reynolds, the Braselton family, John A. Williams, Ronnie Spillers, James Merritt, members of Wayne Mason's prayer group at the 1818 club, and family office members Lori Schoenfuss, Marty Kennedy, and Chris Hayes.

# Index

Abrams, Stacy, 126
ad valorem tax, 66–67. *See also* taxes
agricultural industry, 12, 13, 23
Allen, Robert, 18
*All in the Family* (television show), 78
Ameritech Corporation, 84–85
Archer, Julian, 43
Arlington Capital, 53
arts and culture, 98–99
Atlanta, 3–4, 31, 35, 40–41, 45–46
Atlanta Beltline, 84, 91–96, 97
Atlanta Beltline Inc. (ABI), 94
Atlanta Community Food Bank, 102
*Atlanta Constitution* (newspaper), 21
Atlanta Regional Commission (ARC), 40
automobiles, 22–23, 29–30, 37–38
Autry, Gene, 22
Bagwell, Paula, 99
Bailey, Frank, 37
Bank of America (formerly, Heritage Bank), 52
Barnes, Roy, 57–58, 97, 112
Barry Real Estate, 94
Basinger, Kim, 84
Basinger, Mick, 84
Bell Aircraft (later, Lockheed), 27, 34
Beltline Atlanta, 84, 91–96, 97
Bender, Barbara, 33
Benefield, John William, Jr. ("J. W."), 68–69
"birthing and burying" development model, 87–91
Black Creek Scout Reservation, 105
Board of Commissioners, Gwinnett County (GCC); composition of, 41–46; diversity and, 128; housing challenges, 67–68; Jimmy's role in, 41–42; school redistricting, 128–129; taxes, 66–67; Wayne's role in, vi, 4–5, 43, 50, 58–59, 70
Bolling, Bill, 102
Bona Allen Tannery (harness and saddle factory), 18, 22
*Bonanza* (television show), 22
bootlegging (moonshine running), 37–38, 41
Bowen, Edward, 77
Bowen, K. C., 103
Boy Scouts of America, 105
Brack, Elliot, 64–65, 75, 79–80, 97
Brannen, Hubert, 29
Braselton (town), 19, 84–86, 117
*Brown v. Board of Education,* 68
Buchanan, Buck, 8, 18
Buckhead medical building, 96
Buford (Gwinnett County), 17–19, 22, 43, 45
Buford Dam, 33–36. *See also* Lanier, Lake
Buford Hospital, 79
Buford Rock Quarry Prison for Incorrigibles, 36–37
Buice, Maron, 43
Busbee, Mary Beth, 103
Bush, Warren A., 59
business landscape; Gwinnett as good for business, 67; immigration and, 123–124; license system, countywide, 65; transformation of, 74–80
Butler, J. William, 93

Button Gwinnett Hospital, 79
Byrd, Martha, 31
Calloway, Bo, 63
Camp Creek Baptist Church (Lilburn), 24
Carico, David, 118
Carico, James Mason (Jimmy's grandson), 118
cars, 22–23, 29–30, 37–38
Carter, Jimmy, vi, 109, 267
Carville, James, 110–111
census. *See* population
Central of Georgia Railway, 89
Chamber of Commerce, Gwinnett County, xi, 69, 104, 107, 123–124
Chamber of Commerce, Metropolitan Atlanta, 57, 95
change, challenges of, 86, 127
churches, growth of, 103–104. *See also* names of specific churches
Cisco Systems, 99–100
Civil Rights Act (1964), 120
civil rights movement (1960s), 3, 68
Civil War, 7, 13–17
clinics. *See* medical facilities; names of specific facilities
Clinton, Bill, 5, 111
Clower, Emmett, 32–33
Coffee, Peter, 16
Coffee, William, 16
Cole, Daniel C., 37
commercial corridors, development of, 88
Commission, Gwinnett County. *See* Board of Commissioners, Gwinnett County (GCC)
Community Foundation of Northeast Georgia (Gwinnett Foundation Inc.), 101–102
Compact of 1812, 10
Congress; bank bailout, 94–95; Buford Dam, 34–35; tribute to Wayne, 1, 105–108
corruption, 41–46
cotton industry, 12, 13, 23
Couch, Edgar (Jimmy's brother-in-law), 52, 76
Cover, Horace J., 38
Crews, Alton, 69, 79, 101
crime; mass transit and, 72–73; reputation for lawlessness, 36–39, 41, 44
Cross Point Church, 103
Crossroads at Gwinnett, 88
Cunkleton, John, 43
dairy industry, 23
Declaration of Independence, 7, 9, 148n2
"Declaration of Principles" (Lee), 24
Democratic Party, 120, 122, 125–126, 128. *See also* political landscape, Gwinnett County
DeMuth, Mary Ann, 90
desegregation of schools, 62, 68–69
development, Mason bros. career in; activities, extension of, 83–84; beginnings of, 27, 29, 33, 48–50; "birthing and burying" development model, 87–91; impacts of, 74; *See also* real estate
Dillon, Tom, 81
Discover Mills mall (Duluth), 86, 88
diversification; importance of, 23, 74, 135–137; Mason bros. and, 71, 76–77; power of, 52
diversity, 62, 129–130
Dorsey, Hattie, 95
Drakies Plantation, 90
Duke Realty Corporation, 86
Duluth (Gwinnett County), 19
Duluth Hospital, 32
Dye, Harold, 63
economic conditions; history of, 12, 13, 16–20, 21–23;

interstate, impacts of, 47; 1970s oil shocks, 78–79; 2008 housing crisis, 94–95, 96; unemployment, 78
Edgefield Holdings, 97
education. *See* schools
Eisenhower, Dwight D., 46
Eisenmann-Schier, Ruth, 38
Electromagnetic Sciences (EMS), 74–75
English, Dan, 117
enslaved labor, 13–14, 148n3
Evans, Alex, 37, 38
Ewing, Harvie, Jr., 49, 113
Fine Arts Center (Lawrenceville), 99
First Baptist Church (Snellville), 103–104
Flynt, Larry, 38–39
food banks, 102
Fort McPherson (East Point), 34
Fosque, Marlene, 128
Fowler, Robert, 101–102
Frances Wood Wilson Foundation, 99
Franklin, Dan, 125
Franklin, Joseph Paul, 38–39
freeport tax, 66–67. *see also* taxes
Friendship Church, 24
Fullerton, Marti Pingrey, 26, 110, 151n13
Fulton County Bank, 52
funeral homes, 52, 76
F. Wayne Hill Water Resource Center, 65
GA 124 (highway), 32–33, 57, 88
GA 316 (University Highway), 47
Garden City Terminal (GPA), 89–90
Garrett, Franklin, 92
GCC. *See* Board of Commissioners, Gwinnett County (GCC)
generosity, 2–3, 100
Georgia General Assembly, 30, 41–46, 56, 105–108
Georgia Gwinnett College (GGC), 104–105
Georgia Local Government Public Works Construction Law, 94
Georgia Ports Authority (GPA), 57, 69–70, 89, 101–102, 124
Georgia State Properties Commission, 57
GGC (Georgia Gwinnett College), 104–105
Gibson, Frank L., 43
Gobey's School (near Sugar Hill), 16
Goldwater, Barry, 120
Goodyear, 29–30
GPA (Georgia Ports Authority), 57, 69–70, 89, 101–102, 124
Grady, Henry, 21–22, 24
Gravel, Ryan, 91–92
Gravvit, Harry, 37
Griffin, Marvin, 37
grocery stores, chain, 71, 76
Gullickson, Nancy, 99
Gunnin, Ray, 43
Gwinnett, Button, 7, 9, 147n1
Gwinnett Community Hospital, 77
Gwinnett Council for the Arts, 99
Gwinnett County; county seat, 11–12; demographics of, 119, 121–122, 125; economic history of, 12, 13, 16–20, 21–23; growing pains, 126, 129; history of, 7–8, 9–11, 31–33, 77; legislative districts, 56; MARTA, resistance to, 73–74; as migration destination, 47–48, 121–126; political landscape, 119–122; reputation, negative, 36–39, 41; transformation of, ix–xi, 1–2, 50, 69–70, 83–89, 98
Gwinnett County Bank, 52, 76

Gwinnett County Commission. *See* Board of Commissioners, Gwinnett County (GCC)
Gwinnett County Recreation Department, 66
Gwinnett County Water and Sewer Authority, 56, 62–63, 65, 70
*Gwinnett Daily News,* 102
Gwinnett Foundation Inc. (Community Foundation of Northeast Georgia), 101–102
Gwinnett Hospital Authority Board, 78
Gwinnett Medical Center, 32, 100, 105
Gwinnett Medical System, 79
Gwinnett Place Mall, 71, 79
Gwinnett Technical Institute, 69, 79–80
Hale, Charlie, 16
Hall, Lyman, 9
Hamil, Tim, 117
Hamilton Bank (Chattanooga), 76
Hampton Island Preserve, 96
Hanna, Frank, 84
Harbin, Isham, 16
Harris, Joel Chandler, 24
Hartsfield, William, 3, 34, 35
Hayes Microcomputers, 75
Henderson, Jim, 64, 145
Heritage Bank (later, Bank of America), 52
Herndon, Alan, 25
highways. *See* road systems
home prices, 51–52
hospitals. *See* medical facilities
housing. *See* real estate
Huckaby, Hank, 26, 151n13
Hudgens, Scott, 99, 104
Hudson, Thomas P., 14
I-78 (US Interstate 78), 32
I-85 (US Interstate 85), 47
industry; cotton, 12, 13, 23; leather, 18, 22; New South ethos and, 21–22; telecommunications, 66–67, 74
infrastructure. *See* transportation; Water and Sewer Authority, Gwinnett County
innovation, technology firms and, 47, 74–75
interstate development plan, 46–47
Isakson, Johnny, 1
Jackson, B. M., 83
Jackson County, 11
Jaqueline Casey Hudgens Center for Arts and Learning, 99
Joan Glancy Hospital, 79
Johnson, John, 22
Johnson, Lyndon B., 120
Kemp, Brian, 125
Kennedy, John F., 49–50
Krist, Gary Steven, 38
Ku Klux Klan, 18
Ladford, Thomas, 37
Landrum, Phil, 26
Lanier, Lake, 35, 60, 62–64. *See also* Buford Dam
Lanier Mountain, 49
Lanier Raw Water Intake (Wayne Mason Water Supply Intake Facility), 108
Lawrenceville (Gwinnett County), 12, 18, 88
Lawrenceville Fine Arts Center, 99
Lawrenceville Medical Center, 79
Lawrenceville Women's Club, 99
lawsuits, 96–97, 140–141
Leadership Gwinnett, 101, 116
leather (tanneries), 18, 22
Lee, Ivy Ledbetter, 24
Lee, James Wideman, 23–24
Lettie Pate Evans Foundation, 99
life lessons, Wayne's, 132–145; on character, 143–145; on conflict, 139–140; on debt, 132–134; on diversification, 135–137; on generosity, 137–138; on relationships, 138–139; on

risk-taking, 142–143; on self-sufficiency, 140–142; on talent, 134–135
Lilburn (Gwinnett County), 19, 24, 65
liquor stores, 77
Lockheed (formerly, Bell Aircraft), 27, 34
Loganville-Lawrenceville (L&L) Railroad, 17
lottery, state, 110
*Low v. Austin* (1872), 67
Mackle, Barbara Jane, 38
Maddox, Lester, 26, 109
Marin, Pedro (Pete), 126
MARTA (Metropolitan Atlanta Rapid Transit Authority), 72–74
Martin, Thomas (lynching victim), 16
Martin, Tom (banker), 80
Mason, Ann Biggers (Wayne's wife), 30, 48, 131–132, 144
Mason, Charles, 148n2
Mason, Ellery James (great-grandfather), 23
Mason, George F., 2, 148n2
Mason, Helen Elizabeth Phillips (Jimmy's wife), 48
Mason, Ida Belle Moore (mother), 27–28
Mason, James Winston (father), 4, 27–28
Mason, Jimmy; birth, 25; character traits, vii–viii, 56; death, 56–58, 80–81, 112; marriage, 48; political career, vi–vii, x, 26, 55–57; retirement, 80; school years, 26, 29; values, 112–113; *See also* Mason brothers (Jimmy and Wayne)
Mason, J. P. (grandfather), 4, 24–25, 108
Mason, Keith (Wayne's son), 5, 90–91, 108–112
Mason, Kim (Wayne's daughter), 117
Mason, Kristy (Wayne's daughter), 117
Mason, Mary Almanza Lee (great-grandmother), 23
Mason, Miles, III, 32, 118
Mason, Miles, Jr. (cousin), 32
Mason, Redmond B., 2
Mason, Tracey (Jimmy's daughter), 5, 112–117, 129–130, 144
Mason, Wayne; on being a Democrat, 122; character traits, vii–viii, x–xi, 70, 143–144; generosity, examples of, 53, 100–105, 137; honors and awards, 105–108; Jimmy's death, impact of, 81–82; on lawsuits, 140–141; marriage, 30, 48; on money, 27, 96, 142; money trouble, 1, 71, 79, 132; philosophy, personal, 70; political career, 55, 58–61, 143–144; school years, 26–30; *See also* life lessons, Wayne's; Mason brothers (Jimmy and Wayne)
Mason (m. Carico), Tina (Jimmy's daughter), 117–118
Mason (m. Ewing), Gaye (sister), 25
Mason (m. Herndon), Winifred (sister), 25
Mason (m. Waters), Teresa (Jimmy's daughter), 117–118
Mason brothers (Jimmy and Wayne); bankruptcy, near, 71; comparison of, vii–viii, 30–31, 48; complementary skills, 49, 55, 63; limits, philosophy on, 155n6; relationship, 31, 48–49, 80, 81–82; Snellville development, 33, 49, 71, 75–78
Mason Brothers Construction Company, 48–49, 51

Mason family; legacy, 108–118; philanthropy, history of, 100–105, 117; and public service, 4–6, 8; roots, 2, 7–8, 26, 32–33, 103, 148n2
Mason Mega Rail, 58
mass transit, resistance to, 73–74. *See also* transportation
Mazzawi, Hugh and Anne, 77–78
McCallum, Vic, 22
McConnell, Mart, 16
medical facilities, 31–32, 77–78, 100. *See also* names of specific medical facilities
Merritt, James, 103
Metropolitan Atlanta Rapid Transit Authority (MARTA), 72–74
Metropolitan Planning Commission (MPC), 40
Michelin Tire Company, 67
migration; Gwinnett as destination for, 47–48, 74; importance of, 62; mass transit and, 71–74; white flight, 48, 68, 74, 121–122
Miller, Zell, x, 5, 26, 57, 109–111, 112
Montague, Terri, 94
moonshine running (bootlegging), 37–38, 41
Moore, Hilliard (uncle), 52
Moore, Oscar (grandfather), 2, 24
Morgan, Bartow, Jr., 53, 104, 105, 112
Morton, C. A., 37
mosque controversy, 126–128
Mountain Park Jaycees, 103
Moyers, Bill, 120
Nash, Charlotte, 4, 108, 124
Nash, Norris, 42, 56
National System of Interstate and Defense Highways (Interstate Act, 1956), 46
Native Americans, 9–11
New South ethos, 16–17, 21–22
Nikolich, Katheryn, 5, 36, 47, 66
Nixon, Richard, 44
Norcross (Gwinnett County), 19, 74
Norfolk Southern, 84, 92–93
Norred, Harvard, 43
Nunn, Sam, vi–viii, 55–56, 109
Obama, Barack, 94–95
Oglethorpe, James Edward, 89
oil shocks (1970s), 78–79
O'Kane, John, 104
Park, Sam, 128
Parker, Gordon, 43
Parks and Recreation Department (Gwinnett County), 66
PATH Foundation, 92
Peachtree Corners (Gwinnett County), 74–75
Pendergast, Mark, 91
Perdue, Sonny, 112
Perry, M. C., 37
philanthropy, 98–105, 117, 138–139
Pippin, John, 75
poker game, robbery at, 59–60
political landscape, Gwinnett County; crime and, 44; legislative districts, 128–129; shift to Republican, 80, 119–122
population, Gwinnett County; demographic shift, 120–126; diversity of, 119, 128–129; growth management, 41–43, 44–45; housing boom, 49–51; railroads and growth, 12, 17–19, 22; pre-World War II, 32; post-World War II, 41, 51; 70s and 80s growth, 48, 71; *See also* migration; transportation
Port of Savannah, 58, 89–91
Presidential Market Center, 88
Preston, Diana, 127

# Index

Primitive Baptist Friendship Church, 2
prisons, 36–37, 41, 43–44
Promina Gwinnett Health System Board, 78
Pruitt, W. R. ("Dudge"), 43, 66
Public Law 566 (Watershed Protection and Flood Prevention), 36–37
public-private partnerships, 69, 93–94
public service, 4–6, 8, 55–57, 108–118
racism, 38–39, 62, 68, 95
Ragen, Joseph E., 43
railroads; abandoned corridors, 91–92; impacts of, 12, 17–19, 22; preservation of depots, 103
Rails to Trails Conservancy, 92
Reagan, Ronald, 121
real estate; boom and bust cycles, 51–52, 74; challenges, 67–68; commercial, 75–76; residential, 48–51; 2008 housing crisis, 94–95, 96; Wayne's philosophy on, 84, 87–88; *See also* development, Mason bros. career in
recessions; 1970s, impacts of, 78–79; 2008 housing crisis, 94–95, 96
Recreation Department, Gwinnett County, 66
Reeves, Gene, 38–39
Republican Party, 44, 63, 80. *See also* political landscape, Gwinnett County
reputation, Gwinnett County; corruption, 41–46; good for business, 67; lawlessness, 36–39, 41
R. H. Allen Tannery, 18
Richmond Air Line (railroad), 17
Riddle, John, 100
Rincon, Benjamin, 124
Rivers and Harbors Act (1946), 34
road systems; development of, 46–48, 86; impacts of, 17, 70; *See also* names of specific roads
Robert W. Woodruff Foundation, 99
Robinson, J. Mack, 76
Rogers, Roy, 22
Ronald Reagan Parkway, 86, 88
Roupe, Anna, 73
Rowe, Frank, 99
Russell, Herman, 138–139
Santa Fe Mall (Duluth), 124
Savannah, Port of, 58, 89–91
Savannah Harbor, 89
Sawyer, Jack, 104
Sawyer, James, 32
schools; district maps, 128–129; investment in, 68–69; taxes and, 47, 66–67
science, technology, engineering, and math (STEM), 69, 99–100
Scientific-Atlanta, 75, 99. *See also* Electromagnetic Sciences (EMS)
Seaboard Air Line Railroad, 17, 18
Sears, Roebuck and Co., 48, 49
secession, 14–15
segregation, 62, 68–69
self-sufficiency, 28, 29, 134–135
sewage system, countywide, 64–65
Sewer Authority, Water and (Gwinnett County), 56, 62–63, 65, 70
Shackelford, Wayne, 45, 52, 61, 66, 103
Shoal Creek Water Filter Plant, 108
Simmons, James P., 14
Simpson, J. Earle, 37
slavery, 13–14, 148n3
Smithsonia (land holdings), 76
Snell, Hugh, 58
Snell, Thomas, 32
Snellville (Gwinnett County); history of, 19, 32–33; Mason

bros. development of, 33, 49, 71, 75–78; Mason family roots, 2, 8, 26, 32–33, 103
Snellville City Council, 55
Snellville High School, 26
Snellville Plaza, 71, 75–76
Sorrels, Charles, 43
Southern Bell, 31, 48
Southern Railroad, 17, 103
South Gwinnett High School, 26, 114
State Route 316 (University Highway), 47
STEM (science, technology, engineering, and math), 69, 99–100
Stephens, Alexander Hamilton, 14
Stephens, John D., 8, 104
St. Luke's Episcopal Church (Atlanta), 102
Story, Earl, 42
Strickland, Alice, 8
Strickland, Clyde and Sandra, 100
success, formula for, 53, 131
Sugar Hill (Gwinnett County), 19
Summit Chase Country Club, 52, 59, 71
Summit Ridge Medical Center for Psychiatry and Addiction Medicine, 79
Sydney Lanier Parkway (I-985), 47
tanneries (leather), 18, 22
taxes; Atlanta Beltline project, 94; development and, 39, 47–48; GCC strategy, 66–67
technology firms and innovation, 47, 74–75
Technology Park Atlanta, 74
"ten dollars" story (on self-sufficiency), 28, 29, 134
Three M Investments, 52
Thurmond, Strom, 120
transportation; Atlanta Beltline, 91–96; mass transit, 71–74; railroads, 12, 17–19, 22; roadways, 46–47, 70; *See also* population, Gwinnett County
Trinity Methodist Church, 23
Truman, Harry, 120
Trump, Donald, 125
Tucker, Alan, 80
Tucker, Richard, 31, 50–51, 53–54, 104
2008 housing crisis, 94–95, 96
"Uncle Remus," (Harris), 24
University Highway (State Route 316), 47
US-78 (Wayne Mason Highway), 105–108
Vandiver, Ernest, 46
The Villages at Global Forum (Gwinnett County), 88–89
Wachovia Bank, 96–97
Walmart, 88
Walton, George, 9
Water and Sewer Authority, Gwinnett County, 56, 62–63, 65, 70
water resources; geography of Gwinnett, 9; inter-county agreements, 50; as key to development, ix–x, 34–35, 36, 68; population growth and, 60–65
Waters, Gary, 117–118
Watershed Protection and Flood Prevention (Public Law 566), 36–37
Wayne Mason Highway (US-78), 105–108
Wayne Mason Water Supply Intake Facility (Lanier Raw Water Intake), 108
Webb, Jones, 114
Webb, Lillian, 48
Webb, Wiley, 15
Weeks, Ray, 99
Weeks Corporation, 85
Western Electric, 66–67, 74
white flight, 48, 68, 74, 121–122

# Index

Willbanks, Alvin, 69
Williams, Carvis P. (cousin), 43, 58, 68
Williams, Sam, 57, 61, 91–92, 95
Williams, S. Courtland (uncle), 27
Williams, Virgil, 52, 76–77, 103–104, 110
Winn, Elisha, 11–12, 18
Winn, Richard D., 14
Winn-Dixie, 76
Wood, John S., 35–36
Woodham, John, 94
Woolard, Cathy, 92
Yellow River Water Reclamation Plant (Lilburn), 65
Zoar Methodist Church, 2

# About the Author

Dr. Catherine M. Lewis is Associate Vice Provost of Museums, Archives & Rare Books, and the University Libraries System; executive director of the Museum of History and Holocaust Education; and professor of history at Kennesaw State University. She is the author, coeditor, or coauthor of fifteen books, including, *The Changing Face of Public History: The Chicago Historical Society and the Transformation of an American Museum* (Northern Illinois University Press, 2005), *Don't Ask What I Shot: How Eisenhower's Love of Golf Shaped 1950s America* (McGraw Hill, 2007), *Memories of the Mansion: The Story of the Georgia Governor's Mansion* with Sandra Deal and Dr. Jennifer Dickey (University of Georgia Press, 2015), *Time to Get Tough: How Cookies, Coffee, and a Crash Led to Success in Business and Life* with Michael Coles (University of Georgia Press, 2018), *Soaring: Eleven Guiding Principles on the Path from Segregation to Success* with Lee Rhyant (University of Georgia Press, 2022), and *Kick Up Some Dust: Lessons on Thinking Big, Giving Back, and Doing it Yourself* with Bernie Marcus (William Morrow, 2022). Dr. Lewis has curated more than forty exhibits for organizations around the nation including Delta Air Lines, the United Way, the Breman Museum, and Augusta National Golf Club. She regularly presents at national and international conferences and serves on numerous boards. In 2018, she was named chair of the Robert T. Jones Jr. Program Advisory Committee, a partnership between Emory University and the University of St. Andrews.